# The Companion CAT

How to Live Up to a Cat's Expectations
—and Get It to Live Up to Yours

## Ernest Dickinson

*Photographs by*
Mimi Forsyth

*Cover design and drawings by*
Roberta Sinnock

*Edited by*
Jackie Isabell

DENLINGER's Publishers, Ltd.
Box 76, Fairfax, Virginia 22030

Library of Congress Cataloging-in-Publication Data

Dickinson, Ernest.
     The companion cat : how to live up to a cat's expec-
tations and get it to live up to yours / Ernest Dickinson ;
edited by Jackie Isabell ; photographs by Mimi Forsyth ;
cover design and drawings by Roberta Sinnock.
         p.  cm.
     Includes bibliographical references.
     ISBN 0-87714-145-2
     1. Cats.  I. Isabell, Jackie.  II. Forsyth, Mimi.  III.
Title.
SF442.D53  1990
636.8—dc20
                                                    90-37213

                                    CIP

# Preface

It is said that there is no zealot like a reformed sinner. So to start with a confession, I spent many years as a cat hater. I subscribed to the stereotyped prejudices: cats are aloof, cold, and self-centered; bird murderers barely out of the jungle; instinctively cunning but unteachable.

One fall afternoon—several years after our beloved standard poodle had died, not to be replaced—I was working in the backyard when a caramel-colored kitten walked up out of nowhere. Seeing the small rangy adolescent, as usual, as a threat to our birds, I stamped my foot and shouted at it, "Get out of here!"

It walked about ten feet away, returned, and showing no fear, looked up at me and meowed. Again, I yelled and stamped my foot, and the kitten made the same appealing overture. I said to myself, "How can I be so mean to that little animal?"

I picked it up. Then a few minutes later, I decided to feed it. That was the beginning of the beginning.

My wife and I would let the kitten stay in the garage for a while. A few days later, we gave it access to our screened-in porch. After the kitten got himself mauled by the cat next door and incurred a whopping veterinary bill, Georgie, as he came to be named, moved inside to stay.

We quickly learned something that is obvious to everyone who knows these animals well; cats respond warmly to love, but unlike dogs, they do not usually lay it on indiscriminately. There are exceptions, of course. Once in a while one finds a mean-spirited cat as there is an occasionally vicious dog. On the other hand, I knew one cat, Trotsky, that went to the other extreme. He would jump into any stranger's arms, climb onto the visitor's shoulders, and wind himself like a scarf around that person's neck, purring rapturously all the while.

We, along with many other cat owners, believed that, unlike dogs, these animals could not be trained or could be taught only with great difficulty. It goes against their independent spirits, or so we assumed. Our poodle had relished training exercises to the point where she had earned her CDX (Companion Dog Excellent) degree, passing advanced tests at dog shows, but this would be out of the question for Georgie.

Soon, this misconception also fell. I discovered that not only our pet but virtually all cats can be taught to be good household citizens, to come when called, to ride peaceably and enjoyably in a car, and to walk on a leash. Owners willing to invest just a little extra time and patience will find that their cats can also be taught to do tricks and will get pleasure from these activities.

This book is addressed to readers who keep their cats indoors—the safest place for cats in today's world—allowing them outside only on a leash. Nevertheless, the book will also be useful to owners who allow their cats to go in and out at will.

*The Companion Cat* is primarily a guide to a firmer bonding and closer understanding between owner and pet. Today's vastly increased indoor togetherness of people and cats has brought new roles for both. Owners have new responsibilities and, at the same time, new opportunities to develop a richer understanding and fun-filled rapport with their cats. But this intimacy does not happen automatically just because pet and owner are under the same roof. For its full development, this bond needs to be worked at. The rewards for doing so make the effort well worthwhile.

"If man could be crossed with the cat, it would improve man, but it would deteriorate the cat." — Mark Twain.

# Acknowledgments

All photographs, except the illustrations of training from pages 49 through 61, are by Mimi Forsyth of Santa Fe, New Mexico. Mimi, who owns four cats, takes photos around the world for leading periodicals and book publishers.

Special thanks are due not only to Mimi but also to the following: Jackie Isabell, my editor, for her invaluable contributions throughout the book; Roberta Sinnock for her creative drawings; Dr. Robert A. Mavian of Millwood Animal Hospital (Millwood, New York) for reviewing the information on health and making important additions; our friends who own cats and provided stories and insights; and most important, my wife, Lorraine, whose editorial judgment and encouragement made the book possible.

"In a cat's eyes, all things belong to cats." — English proverb.

# Contents

Companion cats give a special comfort to the elderly.

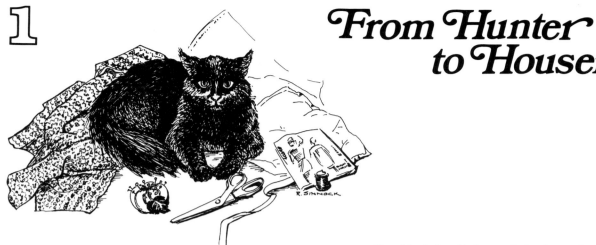

# From Hunter to Housemate

In the United States today, more people are living longer, more people are living alone, and more people are living with cats than ever before. In fact, cats—about 56 million of them—have not only supplanted dogs as America's favorite pets but also, in ever increasing numbers, have moved permanently indoors as household companions.

The relationship between cats and people has changed drastically in just a few generations. In early rural America, Tabby was mostly kept in the barn to catch rats and often had only a nodding acquaintance with the folks up at the house. The shift in the role of cats picked up its greatest momentum between the early 1970s and late 1980s. During that period, the number of people living in cities increased by 33 million, and the number of one-person households doubled to 21 million.

This, of course, is not to say that close companionship with a cat is a new phenomenon. Throughout history, discriminating people have cultivated cat friendships—but in nothing like today's numbers.

Only recently have medical authorities recognized the therapeutic value of a cat's companionship. They have learned that pets can help relieve the loneliness often caused by our society's urbanization and the weakening of family ties.

Charlotte Ebert, a widow who lives in Weyauwega, Wisconsin, says she gets lonely at times, "but my cat family is a great comfort. They ask for so little and give all the love they have in return."

Dr. H. John Geis, a clinical psychologist in New York City, is one of a number in his profession who encourage emotional involvement with a cat, saying it can lead to improved health and happiness. People of all ages, not just the elderly, he says, have a basic need to love and be loved. Although in this respect, a cat does not, of course, equate with a person, a lasting loving relationship with another human being is often an elusive goal, as the divorce rate shows. At any given time, one's temperament, appearance, disability, age, shyness, or some other combination of circumstances may block even an attempt at such a loving relationship—but not so with a pet.

### Tranquilizer in the Lap

The National Institute of Health in Bethesda, Maryland, reports that researchers around the country have learned that pets play a crucial role in promoting people's physical well-being. Patients in wheelchairs, for example, find in pets a source of social stimulation that is often more reliable than that of human companions.

A cat fits nicely in the lap, and few things in life are more calming. Medical experts say that the soothing effects of a cat can reduce blood pressure. In fact, a study of heart attack victims by Dr. Aaron Katcher and Dr. Erika Friedmann of the University of Pennsylvania showed that the death rate among patients with pets was a third less than that of patients with none. Understandably, pet-related therapy programs are springing up in an increasing number of nursing homes, hospitals, psychiatric facilities, and even some prisons.

Few things are more tranquilizing than a cat in the lap. Scientists have documented the medical and psychological benefits of cat companionship.

The Delta Society in Renton, Washington, is a nonprofit public service organization dedicated to furthering the beneficial contacts between people and animals, and it promotes research into the bonding between them. The society reports that it is astonishing what contact with an animal can do for a person's emotional and physical health. For example, simply watching a pet can actually lower stress level and blood pressure.

Significantly, the benefits of the close relationship seem to be reciprocal. Pet cats have a higher resistance to disease and a quicker recovery rate, even when untreated, than feral cats.

In a survey of 961 pet owners, the Army Veterinary Corps found that 71 percent accorded their pet "people" status. In addition, 68 percent placed great importance on the pet in times of depression, 89 percent found themselves being greeted upon coming home, 77 percent found pets understanding them when talked to, and 73 percent said their communication was from pet to owner.

### The Companion of Choice

Today, the preeminent pet of choice for companionship is the cat: Cats have several advantages over dogs as house companions.
- Cats are cleaner
- Cats do not have to be taken outdoors to do their business
- Cats do not bark and jump on guests
- Cats can amuse themselves alone for reasonable periods, although they can come to love attention
- Cats stay in good shape with limited exercise
- Cats are charming, graceful, and decorative

Not that there is anything inherently *wrong* with dogs. Many people love dogs and cats equally. Households that combine one of each generally find that these "natural enemies" readily become pals. Breeds with strong hunting instincts, however, should be introduced to feline friends at an early age.

The loyalty of dogs has always been touted. Faithful Fido is a mythical character—and deserves to be. Unfortunately, many dog lovers tend to underrate the affection of cats. It is true that, unlike dogs, cats typically do not follow people with blind devotion. They discriminate. Humans must deserve a cat's companionship. Unlike a dog or horse, Puss cannot be browbeaten into doing someone's will.

In her essay "Why I Like Cats Better Than Dogs," Dorothy Canfield Fisher wrote that the servility of dogs has a debauching influence on the human ego. She continues:

> If you punish an intelligent, well-brought-up cat who is doing something she knows is wrong, she feels guilty and shows her sense of guilt by a gloomy, depressed bearing (though she never has the remotest idea of feeling any doglike love for you because you have hurt her). But if, out of a clear sky, you mistreat a cat because you happen to feel ill-tempered, she is likely to whirl her supple body about and bite you. More power to her teeth, say I. That's the kind of pet needed by human beings.[1]

By and large, cats love those who give evidence of loving them. The more attention they get the more they respond. Of course, some pets, especially those alienated in the past, may take longer to warm up than others.

The aloofness syndrome can become a self-fulfilling expectation. As long as cats are believed to be uncongenial and are left outdoors on their own and treated coolly, most of them live up to that reputation.

All senses on alert, this hunter plays a waiting game.

11

Mimi Forsyth's Diva, Bear, Marco Polo, and Charlie. One stands guard at night. Each has a distinctive personality.

*Understanding* Felis Domesticus

Understanding of *Felis domesticus* must start with the awareness that each cat has its own unique personality—and the quirks to go with it. To learn how different cats are from each other, one has only to own two or more of them.

Mimi Forsyth of Santa Fe, New Mexico, has four cats. Here is her thumbnail characterization of each:

• *Charlie:* Languid and aloof, but a softy when affectionate. A shoulder-climber. He is the dominant of the household. Proud of his long, silky tail, his plume. Loud purrer.

• *Diva:* Flouncy. Fickle. Doesn't take any guff from anyone. Don't touch her paws. She bites. First to the food, even knocking Charlie out of the way. Finds predicaments and gets into them, crawling into spaces too small. Very vocal but seldom purrs.

• *Marco Polo:* Dignified, wise, reserved. Easily embarrassed. Allows cuddling only when no one else is around. Never a hair out of place. My guardian. He senses my moods and is responsive. Never purrs.

• *Bear:* Not as smart as the others but the most outgoing. Always first to the door when the bell rings. Allows himself to be cuddled by even total strangers. Knows who doesn't like cats and goes straight to that lap. Purrs constantly.

From the time they are able to walk, kittens are incurably nosey—a sure sign of intelligence.

Eccentric as each cat may be, underlying its individuality are certain common traits. Independence of character is one of them. For example, a cat—when it is ready to so honor you—will leap into your lap, curl up, and usually purr blissfully. Just as abruptly, when the impulse comes to check out its food dish or to investigate a faint rustle in the next room—thump! Your friend has jumped down and is gone.

It may seem contradictory but, despite this compulsion to do its own thing, a cat can be happily trained to come when called, to ride in a car, and to perform certain tricks, which are described in later chapters. However, the teaching must be done *only* with love, praise, and treats—never by coercion. Even then, a cat's education has certain natural limits. For example, although a cat will learn to walk with a harness and leash, it will insist on pausing from time to time to look around; it will not heel in a straight line, military fashion, as a dog will.

Nosiness is another dominant feline characteristic. The old saying that "curiosity killed the cat" has its basis in truth. A friend of ours was about to stuff her Thanksgiving turkey when she found her kitten had crawled into the cavity. The little explorer was pulled out, of course, in time to save it from the oven. A cat must investigate every nook and cranny of a new environment, again a sign of intelligence. It explores with ears, eyes, nose, and paws. The cat's memory records every detail of information. In addition, any time an empty box is put down, a file drawer pulled out, or a closet door opened a crack—just enough for a claw to pry at it—Chief Inspector Tabby will go to work.

### The Cat Stands Guard

Stories of dogs defending their masters and their households are legion, but cats seem to some extent to have protective instincts too. Of course, they do not scare away intruders with a bark, but they have hearing keen enough to alert them to suspicious activities.

Mimi Forsyth tells how every night three of her cats sleep on her bed upstairs while a fourth takes guard duty downstairs napping on the couch by the front door. Mimi does not know how they decide which one is to be sentinel, but whatever the system, they rotate the chore. "They've never yet had to warn me of any real emergency," she says, "but the three on the bed frighten me now and then, when they all of a sudden will sit bolt upright and stare at the bedroom door. I think they hear ghosts."

Rita Bott of Pinellas Park, Florida, is convinced it was not a ghost that her cat heard in the middle of the night. "When Dixie jumped on me howling and sounding terribly alarmed," Rita says, "I remember looking at my digital clock beside the bed and noticing that it was 1:59 in the morning. The cat kept leaping on and off the bed, crying and running around the room." Rita got up. She checked everything she could think of, even brought in a fan because she thought the cat might be hot. Nothing did any good. About twenty minutes later, Dixie subsided and fell asleep. "The next morning when I went outside, I saw that my car that had been parked beside the house where I always keep it was gone," she says. "The police finally found it and the kids who had taken it for a joyride. They said they had stolen it about 2:00 in the morning." Rita says she is sure that Dixie was trying to alert her that something out of the ordinary was going on next to the house.

Jean Seddon of Santa Rosa, California, has no doubt that her twenty- five-pound Siamese, Jeremy, would actually attack a burglar or any other intruder. When a house painter came inside to use the telephone, Jeremy crouched low in his attack mode, growled, and started after him. Jean chased her pet and scooped him up before he could do bodily damage. "I'm sure Jeremy would have liked to have shredded him," she says. "He was protecting the house."

Even Big Brother loves his catnap.

### Not a Workaholic

Of course, if there is one thing the cat is not, it is a workaholic. It does only what it considers needs to be done—like washing up every twenty minutes—then settles down to enjoy life in its own placid way. The cat is a model of efficiency and energy conservation. It makes few wasted motions. Unlike the dog, it does not run about aimlessly or bark at shadows by the hour, and it sees no point at all in chasing a stick and bringing it back time after time. William Lyon Phelps wrote that every household should have a cat, not just for decorative and domestic values but as a calming influence on irritable, tense, and restless men and women. Phelps noted that when the cat "decides to take his repose, he not only lies down; he pours himself onto the floor like water. It is restful merely to behold him."[2]

Repose is something a cat takes seriously. An editorial writer in *The New York Times,* poking fun at a cat's day, described it as "a 20-hour snooze, 10 minutes pushing a bottle cap across the floor and one minute spitting up a hairball."[3] The observation was not far off the mark. Cats sleep an average of fifteen hours a day, far more than most mammals.

The contentment flag is up. For the moment, at least, Puss is at peace with the world.

## Well-Equipped by Nature

Nature has given the cat a set of faculties well-suited to its role in life.

A cat can hear sounds up to sixty thousand cycles a second; the human ear picks up noises only to twenty thousand. About twenty different muscles for each ear shell enable a cat to move one ear independently of the other. The combination of head movement with flexing of the ears allows the cat to scan an area and pinpoint a sound source quickly. Acute hearing explains why Tabby, even when ap-

pearing to be in a deep sleep, can detect the sound of a refrigerator door opening three rooms away—not to mention the footfall of a mouse. Two Siamese cats at the Dutch embassy in Moscow in 1964 kept scratching at the walls and meowing. Believing there were mice inside, the staff had the walls opened. What the cats had heard were the delicate workings of Russian microphones hidden there for bugging purposes.

In some respects, cats also see better than people do. In dim light, their eyes are half again more efficient than those of human beings, and their field of vision is much broader. A cat does have some visual limitations. It has poor perception of nearby stationary objects. It also has only a fraction of the human eye's capacity for color distinction. The world in which a cat lives is believed to be mostly black, gray, and white, although it can distinguish blue and yellow.

Cats sleep an average of fifteen hours a day, far more than most mammals.

15

When the ears are down, better back off and leave Kitty alone.

Cats are expert at judging distance. Just watch your pet gauge the height of a table or bureau before jumping up. If the cat does fall, it is usually only because of a slippery doily or something else on the upper surface not visible from the floor.

Some of the aura of mysticism that has clung to the cat over the centuries may be attributed to its eyes. First, cats have an unnerving tendency to stare at people without blinking; and second, cats' eyes at times glow in the dark. When a beam of light is suddenly cast on a cat before its pupils have time to contract, a mirrorlike layer on the retina reflects the light in such a way that the eyes turn into two eerily glowing orbs.

The cat's acute sense of smell is used in the selection and appreciation of food. This may compensate somewhat for the fact that its sense of taste is more muted than ours. A cat's taste buds are found only on three parts of the tongue, whereas taste

In low light, a cat can see 50 percent more than humans, but its color perception is not as good.

buds virtually cover the tip, sides, and back of the upper surface of the human tongue.

The cat's sense of smell picks up territorial markings. A male sprays around its territory to warn off other cats. Both males and females rub their heads against a person or a piece of furniture to mark it as their own with scent from the glands on the sides of their heads.

In addition to its unique ways of hearing, seeing, and smelling, Tabby has a vocal repertoire too extensive to catalog. There are mews, meows, mrows, yowls, howls, and hisses of all tones and intensities and other sounds besides. For example, when our Georgie spots birds from his window seat, he makes a distinctive soft hunting cry that has been likened to the creak of a rusty hinge. One soon begins to recognize the insistent calls for dinner that, if ignored, can turn into a wailing, heart-rending aria, translated as "O, starving I!"

Purring is made by vocal cords when the laryngeal passage constricts. It usually denotes contentment, although cats occasionally purr when in pain.

How did cats come to purr? Muriel Beadle, in her book *The Cat,* cites an ancient folk tale that explains it. In order to save her true love from death, a princess was set the task of spinning ten thousand skeins of linen thread in thirty days. She knew this was impossible to do alone, so she asked her three cats to help. They worked day and night and finished the task in the allotted time. As a reward, cats were given the ability from then on to make the whirring sound of the spinning wheel.

### All This and Body Language Too

A cat uses its entire body as well as its voice to express itself. Rubbing, for example, is used as a means of communication. When a cat wants to be fed, just watch it do a snake dance around your legs.

A cat that carries its tail straight up is usually signaling happiness. However, when the tail starts to swish, watch out. That lashing often means irritability. If the ears lay back and down, that is an even more urgent signal to back off and leave Puss alone. Cats, like people, now and then have dark moods that should be respected.

Kittens that are raised indoors have predatory instincts but lack the barnyard skills taught by their mother.

Kneading, on the other hand, is usually a sign of contentment. The cat presses first one paw and then the other against your body or some other soft object while extending and retracting its claws. This is a reversion to kittenhood when it nursed, using this method to stimulate the flow of milk.

### Hunting Skills Vary

At one time, virtually all of the cat's unique faculties were utilized in hunting. Today, the predatory instinct seems to vary widely from one animal to another, even among members of the same family, and many modern indoor cats are not nearly as good mousers as their ancestors. This may be partly because the present feline generation is pampered and better fed, and there may be fewer mice around to catch. More important, most kittens nowadays do not have the opportunity to go out in the field and learn hunting techniques from their mothers as they once did.

Cats on the prowl in the wild had many opportunities to scratch on the trunks of trees. Scratching is a natural instinct. This activity helps cats to stretch their muscles and to peel off old claw sheaths so that sharp new claws underneath can emerge.

### A Prehistoric Family

The fact that some people have ambivalent feelings about cats is not surprising. In part, this may reflect an atavistic sense of mystery about these animals. From the earliest times, mankind's attitude toward cats has varied from veneration in some cultures to fear and hatred in others, but superstition has followed the cat wherever it has gone. Considering the cat's stealth and habit of nocturnal roaming, it is not surprising that people should associate this creature with the supernatural.

With its glowing eyes and nocturnal wanderings, the cat has retained its aura of mystery and superstition for centuries.

Researchers believe the feline family dates back possibly forty million years, predating both humans and dogs. As cats adapted to different hunting environments, about three-hundred types evolved, such as leopards, ocelots, wildcats, jaguars, and pumas. All cats became stalking animals, relying on cunning and secrecy to capture their prey.

Egyptians first domesticated cats from a wild north African species about five thousand years ago. Originally kept to rid grain storehouses of rats and mice, cats were eventually proclaimed sacred by Egyptian priests. The cat goddess, Bastet (also called Bast or Pasht), looked over them. The earliest temple portrait of Bastet is dated about 3000 B.C. By 950 B.C., Bastet had become the most powerful of all Egyptian goddesses.

Archaeologists have found about 300,000 mummified cats in Egypt as well as countless sculpted, carved, or molded images of cats in all kinds of postures and materials, ranging from clay, glass, stone, and agate to bronze, silver, and gold.

When family cats died, owners shaved their eyebrows as a sign of mourning. To kill a cat brought punishment by death. It is said that when the Persians attacked Egypt, these enemy soldiers carried cats as armor. The Egyptians could not fight back without risk of harming their sacred animals.

Cats were smuggled onto ships leaving Egypt to kill the rats on board. Thus, cats made their way to Greece, Rome, and other countries and eventually to Europe, where the cat population grew rapidly.

*Witchcraft's Terrible Toll*

During the Middle Ages, European cats fell on evil days because Christian leaders associated them with pagan religions, devils, and witches. Witchcraft trials represented cats to be demons. From the concept that a witch could transform herself into a cat nine times, there evolved the superstition that a cat has nine lives. The mysterious doings of the cat, Pywacket, in the play *Bell, Book and Candle* by John Van Druten, show that the idea of a cat as a witch's "familiar" persists in literature.

Throughout Europe, the extent of religious persecution of cats and the cruelty involved are now hard to even imagine. Cats by the millions perished from being tortured, burned, or otherwise killed. For example, the ashes of cats burned alive in St. John's Day bonfires were distributed as good luck charms. Throwing cats off church belfries on religious holidays, it was believed, helped purge the towns of evil.

The British paid for their slaughter of cats with the Black Plague outbreak of 1664. By then, there were not enough cats left in England to keep the rat population from exploding and spreading the bubonic plague through their fleas.

By the mid-1600s, France was leading the way toward cats' gradual return to favor in Europe. Cats began to appear in French art and literature, and notables such as Cardinal Richelieu, who kept many cats at court, helped make them fashionable.

Religious persecution of cats never developed in China and Japan. In fact, for several hundred years after the Japanese introduced cats from China in the tenth century, only noble families could own them, and these pets were revered. Since then, generations of Japanese artists have celebrated the grace and mystery of cats in drawings, paintings, bronze, and ivory.

One would like to write a happy ending to these few historical notes, but it would be misleading to imply that all now goes well for cats around the world. In some of the poorest communities in Asia, Latin America, and elsewhere, cats not only suffer along with people but become items on the *plat du jour*.

## Famous Cat Lovers—and Haters

Since ancient Egypt, cats have never enjoyed the widespread popularity as companions that they do today; yet, as far back as Mohammed's cat, Muezza, there have always been men and women who treasured and kept these animals at their sides. The number includes famous writers, artists, statesmen (even American presidents, the most recent being Jimmy Carter), and religious leaders.

Among the religious leaders, for example, was Pope Leo XII. One of his cats, Micetto, born in the Vatican, had the run of the Sistine Chapel. Eventually, the pope gave Micetto to French author and statesman Chateaubriand, who had seen and fallen in love with it.

Dr. Samuel Johnson had a favorite cat named Hodge. James Boswell, Johnson's biographer, wrote, "I shall never forget the indulgence with which he treated Hodge, his cat, for whom he, himself, used to go out and buy oysters lest the servants, having that trouble, should take a dislike to the poor creature."[4]

Cats captivated the nineteenth-century French author Theophile Gautier. In *La Menagerie Intime,* he wrote about his companion cats that included Don Pierot de Navarre, Childebrand, Zizi, Cleopatre, and others, but he had one favorite:

Madame-Theophile, a red cat, with a white breast, pink nose, and blue eyes, so called because she lived with me on a footing of conjugal intimacy. She slept on the foot of my bed, snoozed on the arm of my chair while I was writing, came down to the garden and accompanied me on my walks, sat at meals with me, and not infrequently appropriated morsels on the way from my plate to my mouth.[5]

Cats and writers seem to have had a particular affinity. The list of other authors who loved these animals includes Baudelaire, Anatole France, Victor Hugo, Emile Zola, Montaigne, Samuel Butler, the Bronte sisters, Thomas Hardy, Mark Twain, Edgar Allen Poe, Henry James, John Keats, and William Wordsworth.

The grace and beauty of cats have beguiled artists. Among those who have portrayed them in their work were Rembrandt, Da Vinci, Renoir, and Picasso. The lesser-known Swiss artist Gottfried Mind made a career of painting cats.

By contrast, some notables have disliked cats intensely. Sixteenth-century French poet Pierre de Ronsard, for example, claimed nobody hated a cat more than he did. He wrote, "I hate their eyes, their faces, their stares." He went on—

I detest those fools who can't survive
  Without a cat staying nearby.
  Nonetheless, this dreadful creature
  Comes to lie close by my head,
  Invading the softness of my downy pillow.

*("Le Chat")*

Others who shared Ronsard's antipathy include Alexander the Great, Louis XIV, Napoleon, and Julius Caesar.

Boswell, Johnson's biographer, even while recording his subject's devotion to Hodge, wrote that he himself was uneasy in a room with a cat and often "suffered a good deal from the presence of this same Hodge."[6]

Today, America has its share of people who still have not succumbed to feline charms. For example, Mark Patinkin, *Providence Journal* syndicated columnist, sees the numerical ascendancy of cats over dogs as a "grim development." He writes—and, perhaps, only half in jest—that he is among those who believe if cats were bigger they would eat people "instead of those little tins" of food, adding that "the way cats stare at people makes them a leading cause of mental illness in the United States."[7]

A champion cat hater in Chicago specified in his will that boxes of candy be sent to 150 other people who felt as he did.

Such aelurophobes may have been hard to find because cat veneration is on the increase. Owners nowadays do not shave their eyebrows when their pets die, but many mourn the loss as a death in the family. In one survey of cat owners, 65 percent said they thought cats were easier to get along with than most people, and 43 percent said the principal reason for their getting a cat was loneliness. It is little wonder that Americans spend $1.4 billion a year for about a million tons of cat food and $89 million on cat-box litter, to say nothing of veterinary bills, toys, carriers, cat books, cat calendars, cat bumper stickers—and tickets to the Broadway musical *Cats.*

Cats keep each other company, an asset for owners who must be absent for long periods of time.

# 2 *First Considerations*

Caring for a cat, though far easier than a dog, still brings responsibilities that should be considered ahead of time. The new owner should have the quarters, the capability, the time, and the temperament to care for a pet adequately and lovingly. Unfortunately, some people decide on impulse to get a cat. They do not foresee complications that could cause them to give up the animal a short time later, often with a disturbing effect on both pet and owner.

What are potential causes of trouble?
- A landlord who objects
- A housemate who dislikes cats
- A work schedule that does not allow enough time with the cat
- Costs that may prove burdensome, especially for an older person living on a fixed income

There may be a chance that through advance discussion a landlord, spouse, or other companion could be persuaded to make an accommodation.

Becoming a cat owner who is absent most of the day can raise problems. A cat is by nature a solitary animal. Given some toys and a window perch with a view of the outdoors, it can be left alone for reasonable periods of time, much of which will be spent snoozing, which is why many people decide to get a cat instead of a dog. However, cats that are kept indoors, as they should be (a subject covered later in this chapter), do have some special requirements. Indoor cats are deprived of the stimula-

tion of change of scene, exploration, and adventure that outdoor life provides, so they need at least a minimal amount of human or animal company to avoid boredom.

Veterinarians say that, although indoor cats have fewer medical problems than their outdoor counterparts, confined single animals that are regularly left to themselves for most of the day tend to develop behavioral problems. On the other hand, cats or kittens have a large capacity for finding interest and entertainment in one another. Therefore, people who are absent for long periods of time should consider acquiring a pair of pets. Single cat owners who are away even intermittently should spend some time before and after the absence giving their cat extra attention and affection.

The cost of food and routine medical care for a cat is usually not a hardship, even for people of modest means. Yet for some senior citizens on a low fixed income, who may be the most lonely and the most in need of a pet's company, that expense could be an important factor.

## Making Adoption Easier

Among a variety of programs around the country that make it easier for senior citizens to adopt pets, probably the most extensive is Purina's Pets for People Program. Nationwide, it has enabled more than fifteen thousand men and women sixty years and older to adopt either a cat or dog at no initial cost. More than one hundred shelters in metropolitan areas across the country administer the program the year around, and another eighty-eight take part in August and September each year.[8]

Ralston Purina Company pays participating

shelters $100 for each pet adopted, up to ten animals a month. This sum, except in rare cases, covers all the costs of acquiring the pet, including the initial veterinary care, inoculations, spaying/neutering, and office visits for the first two weeks. Purina gives the new owner, in addition, a starter food supply, collar, leash, and feeding bowl as well as free literature and guidance in proper pet care.

The applicant's income is not an eligibility factor, but those applying are screened to make sure they are able to give the pet proper ongoing care, either alone or with the help of relatives or friends. Applicants do not have to live in the city where the shelter is located.

Volunteers provide counseling for people with new pets. They help select the right one for the right person and make follow-up phone calls to be certain the new owner and pet are getting along well. "We see instant love when we match seniors and pets," says Larry Boersma of the San Diego Humane Society. "The staff members really feel good about the program and the benefits to our shelter and to senior citizens."

Aside from the Purina program, many individual shelters have their own assistance plans to encourage the bonding of older people and pets. San Francisco's Society for the Prevention of Cruelty to Animals (SPCA), for example, has an extensive senior services program funded by contributions. Here, pet owners over sixty-five who need special assistance can obtain it in many forms such as free pet coupons, pet food delivery, a pet health care plan, and pet transportation to the SPCA hospital when no other is available.

In the communities of Cape Cod, Martha's Vineyard, and Nantucket, the Sampson Fund in East Dennis, Massachusetts, provides financial help for sick or injured companion animals that need veterinary care their owners cannot afford. The fund is financed solely by membership fees and donations.

### Indoors or Out?

When acquiring a kitten or cat, owners should decide whether the animal will have free access to the outdoors or whether it will be a strictly indoor pet. The case for keeping a cat indoors nowadays is overwhelmingly persuasive. It is also one with which many veterinarians agree.

Some cat owners who let their pets roam believe that confining a cat is cruel. Not only is that not true, given reasonable indoor conditions, but also research shows that indoor cats are healthier and safer than those allowed outdoors and that they live an average of six-to-seven years longer. Most indoor cats live into their teens; few outdoor ones do.

Many people believe that cats, perhaps because of their jungle image, can hunt and survive nicely on their own in the wild. The truth is just the opposite. Cats, particularly in our present-day urban/suburban environment, rely more than ever on people to nurture, shelter, and protect them.

Nor is it true that cats need to run about in the great outdoors. They require only a fraction of the exercise that a dog does because cats are not by nature running animals. Their instinct is to resort to stealth, the lie-in-wait pause, and the quick pounce. Also, no matter where the cat is, it spends the greater part of its day napping.

Cats love games that simulate hunting. They rely on stealth, lie-in-wait, and the quick pounce.

Consider, then, the advantages of keeping a cat indoors. It avoids:
• Death by being hit by a car (and possibly causing an auto accident for a driver trying to avoid it)
• Poisonings—accidental or otherwise
• Injuries from fights with other cats and the resulting veterinary bills
• Contracting and spreading contagious diseases
• Picking up fleas and ticks and bringing them indoors
• Contributing to ecological damage by killing birds

The number of outdoor cats succumbing to indirect poisoning seems to be large and increasing—a danger not sufficiently recognized. Mice or rats poisoned by householders often stagger outside for water before dying and may be eaten by neighborhood cats. The widespread use of pesticides by farmers poisons both birds and mice—and, by accident, often the cats that devour them.

Given the proper attention, indoor cats become well-adjusted and happy. They also tend to become more people oriented and make more congenial companions. Then, too, the owner of an indoor pet has a greater opportunity to enjoy the cat, to watch its graceful movements and charming antics.

*Making the Choice*

People, of course, acquire cats in many ways. Like the finding of a mate, the process is not always deliberate. For example, the cat may be a foundling. More accurately, *you* may be the foundling, which is to say, a stray cat may have found and sized you up as a soft touch.

Once people develop a warm spot in their hearts for cats, they sometimes find it impossible to resist any cat that is in trouble. Such self-styled softies are Dave and Sharon Crider of Superior, Arizona.

"It was sleeting on Christmas Eve in 1967," says Sharon. "We had driven to our local grocery store for a few last-minute items. As we were walking into the store, Dave noticed a half-starved black-and-white kitten licking moisture off the outdoor Coke machine. Our home already had 12 cats in it. It was 'impossible' to add another. But when I came out of the store I saw Dave already had the kitten nestled inside his goose-down vest." Bismark, as this pet

People with a fondness for animals—like these youngsters—find it almost impossible to resist a kitten.

came to be called, was so weak he could not retain his first meal, but he soon recovered his health and joined the Crider ménage.

Another of the Crider's cats, Gretchen, had lived under a chicken coop. The farmer asked David, who is a police officer, to get rid of the cat "one way or another." David finally lured Gretchen out. The cat had barely survived for months on a diet of the corn fed to the chickens, and she had developed so strong a taste for corn that even after she regained her health, it remained her favorite food.

Sharon rescued a third Crider cat. "I was driving our pick-up in a torrential rain in San Bernardino," she says. "When I stopped at a left-turn signal, I glanced out the side window and saw a tiny kitten being swept along the gutter towards a storm drain." Sharon pulled to the curb and ran across two lanes of traffic, reaching the storm drain just in time to save the kitten from drowning. "She is now the grande dame of our house," Sharon says.

In a survey by *Cat Fancy* magazine, 36 percent of the respondents said their animals came to them as strays. There is nothing new about this, of course. Harriet Beecher Stowe's Maltese cat, Calvin, simply walked into her house one day out of nowhere and looked up at her as if to say, "I've come to live with the author of *Uncle Tom's Cabin*."

*Where to Get Your Pet*

Assuming you have a choice in the selection, where would you go to make it?

Adopting a cat from the local shelter gives the added satisfaction of knowing you are probably saving it from being put to death. Of the about twelve million cats that enter shelters each year, more than nine million are euthanized. The shelter's required examinations and inoculations will likely insure getting a healthy animal.

Occasionally, one can make an exceptionally lucky find at a shelter. Betti Trestman of Phoenix, Arizona, picked out a kitten with unusually pretty markings. When she later saw a newspaper article about Ocicats, she suspected her kitten might be one of that breed and did some detective work. An eastern breeder of Ocicats had given the kitten to a friend, who was driving back to California. By Phoenix, the friend had decided a kitten was too much trouble and simply dropped it off at the shelter. Betti obtained the kitten's papers and is now an active breeder.

Other options would be to get your pet from a professional breeder, from a friend or neighbor who might have kittens, from a classified ad placed by someone looking for a good home for kittens, or from a pet shop.

If you are among those deciding to get a purebred cat and are not already knowledgeable on the subject, it would be prudent to do some research first. For example, Cat Fanciers Association (CFA) will supply a leaflet on the particular breed being considered, with information about temperament and distinguishing physical characteristics, free of charge.[9] Cat magazines, cat shows, breed clubs, and veterinarians can also help familiarize prospective owners with purebreds. Ask the librarian at the public library for help finding books and articles on the subject. Those books not available locally can usually be obtained through the interlibrary loan network.

"The first rule in shopping for a purebred cat is 'buyer beware,'" says Lois Gambos, spokesperson for CFA.

Our association has more than 25,000 breeders registered with us. We cannot police them all. The buyer should inspect the cattery. At least make sure it looks clean and the cats appear healthy. Ask for a reference or two. Try to obtain in writing from the breeder an agreement that if your veterinarian does not find the animal to be healthy upon examination, you can return it for a refund. And never leave without the official registration application in your hand. Do *not* let anyone tell you, 'we will mail it to you later.'

## Breeds Registered by the Cat Fanciers Association, Inc.

| | | |
|---|---|---|
| Abyssinian | Cymric | Ocicat |
| American Shorthair | Devon Rex | Persian* |
| American Wirehair | Egyptian Mau | Oriental Shorthair |
| Balinese | Exotic Shorthair | Rissian Blue |
| Birman | Havana Brown | Scottish Fold |
| Bombay | Japanese Bobtail | Siamese |
| British Shorthair | Javanese | Singapura |
| Burmese | Korat | Somali |
| Chartreux | Maine Coon | Tonkinese |
| Colorpoint Shorthair | Manx | Turkish Angora |
| Cornish Rex | | |

* Includes the following divisions: Himalayan, Particolor, Shaded, Smoke, Solid, Tabby.

The joy of watching a kitten at play has few equals.

Common domestic shorthaired kittens are often advertised as being free to a good home. Shorthaired cats are much easier to care for than longhaired ones because the latter require frequent grooming.

Buying a cat from a pet shop may be the least attractive option. Many of these stores are reputable, but others have animals that are bred by virtual cat factories. Buyers run a risk of getting a pet that has been neglected and is weak and possibly diseased.

### Kit or Cat

Should you choose a grown cat or a kitten? Each has its advantages.

An older person may find a more sedate, mature cat a better choice than a kitten. The latter is a world-class mischief-maker day or night, and it is also treacherous underfoot. Others may prefer the youngster. The joy of watching a kitten bouncing about in play may more than compensate for the inconveniences. Most mature cats, even if initially aloof, eventually do come around. Unless they have been traumatized, cats generally form happy relationships with loving new owners.

But one warning. If planning to keep a cat exclusively as an indoor companion, you may be asking for problems by adopting a grown one that has habitually had access to the outdoors. Its adjustment to confinement may be difficult. An old roamer, remembering its days of freedom, can make life miserable by being constantly on the lookout for a way to squeeze out the door or to jump out a window that has been left ajar. Troublesome though it may be, the transition from outdoor to indoor life *can* be accomplished.

### What to Look for

In choosing a kitten, find out, if possible, the characteristics of the mother. Also, kittens that have been fondled and socialized at an early age are often

25

more affectionate than those left entirely alone. Pick one that seems playful and outgoing, not listless or withdrawn. Preferably a kitten should be at least two months old, weaned, and housebroken.

Of course, if one is adopting a cat from a shelter, it may be unreasonable to expect it to take to strangers at once. In addition, the cat's recent misadventures may have made it insecure and frightened.

Whatever the cat's age, look for cleanliness about the eyes and nose, with both free of any mucus discharge. Drooling, coughing, or sneezing means illness. A distended belly on a kitten usually means worms. Open the kitten's or cat's mouth. There should be no redness, and the teeth should be white, the gums pink. Look in the ears. A dark, congealed substance there usually indicates ear mites.

To avoid a chance of heartbreak later, tell whomever you are obtaining the cat from that you are accepting it on condition that it passes an examination by a veterinarian. No matter how or from whom a cat is acquired, it should either have had all the necessary inoculations or should get them as soon as possible.

### Selecting a Name

If your cat comes with no name or with one not to your liking, the possibilities are endless. Perhaps because they are such mystery-laden creatures, cats tend to inspire more exotic names than dogs do. Mark Twain called his cats Sour Mash, Apollinaris, Blatherskite, and Zoroaster. This, Twain wrote, tongue in cheek, was "to practice the children in large and difficult styles of pronunciation." He added that the cats "died early on account of being so overweighted by their names—it was said."[10] Author Frank Swinnerton christened his pets Honorable Fiddledeedee, Mrs. Gummidge, and Tippety-wicket. Queen Victoria had her White Heather and President Carter, his Misty Malarkey. In T. S. Eliot's *Old Possum's Book of Cats,* we find such colorful monickers as Rum Tum Tiger, Macavity, Old Deuteronomy, Skimbleshanks, Mr. Mistoffelees, and that stoutest of cats Bustopher Jones.

Not all literary cats have fancy names. Charles Dickens called his pet William, but when it had kittens, he changed it to Williamina.

If you want to join the mainstream, the most common names for females in the United States are Samantha, Misty, Patches, Calico, Muffin, Angel, Ginger, Tiger, Princess, and Pumpkin. For tomcats, strangely, Tom does not make the top ten, which are Tiger, Smoky, Pepper, Max, Simon, Morris, Mickey, Rusty, Boots, and Charlie.

If you pick a long name for your cat, use a shortened version for calling it. A London puss named Oliver Cromwell, for example, becomes Olly, and Dr. Cuddles becomes Doc. This makes name recognition and training much easier.

### Spaying and Neutering

Each year, about twenty million dogs and cats are brought to shelters and SPCAs, and almost nine out of ten of these animals are euthanized or donated to research laboratories. More than half a billion

Kittens that have been fondled and socialized are often more affectionate than those left alone.

"Say AH!" A healthy cat should have no redness about the mouth. The teeth should be white and the gums pink.

dollars in municipal funds and donations are required to catch, house, and dispose of this surplus animal population.

Cats, because they are prolific breeders and because so many of them are abandoned after they have outgrown their kitten charms, pose a greater problem than dogs. Besides those animals that are collected and euthanized, another five-to-ten million strays suffer worse fates as victims of disease, hunger, or highway death.

A typical shelter spays or neuters cats that are old enough before releasing them to new owners. For kittens too young for the surgery, the adoption fee often includes the cost of this operation, and the new owner agrees to bring the cat back for the surgery.

Unfortunately, most neuter incentive programs offered by shelters and adoption agencies do not work well because so many owners neglect to return with their pets or they let their cats breed first. So it is essential that a pet owner have the animal spayed or neutered.

Conventional wisdom sets six months of age as the best time for neutering, although recent research suggests that altering at an earlier age may eventually be deemed feasible.

A low-cost spaying and neutering clinic can perform the operation safely at a fraction of what a private practitioner typically charges. The clinics are established to do only this surgery and to do it in large numbers. Some units are privately or publicly subsidized, so they can pass along the savings. Most clinics do not have any income criterion, and they serve all comers. Anyone who finds it a hardship to pay for even the clinic's low-cost surgery should ask the local shelter about the possibility of help. Sometimes a subsidy is available for the needy. Ask the local shelter or humane society where the nearest clinic can be found, or mail an inquiry to the Animal Protection Institute of America.[11]

Cats enjoy playing around plants. They occasionally nibble on greenery, so be sure to remove poisonous household plants when a cat joins the family.

Your regular veterinarian, of course, can perform these operations, but ask for a list of *specific* charges. Some veterinarians quote one price for the surgery and may or may not mention additional fees for anesthesia and postoperative care that sometimes triple the expense. Spaying and neutering fees vary among doctors, and shopping around often yields considerable savings. The fee for neutering a male begins at about $25, and many clinics discharge the animal as soon as it has recovered from anesthesia. The average spaying fee is about $55, and postoperative care, which might not be included in the fee, is more likely to be recommended; in such a case, the owner may be handed a bill for as much as $150.

Owners find that an altered animal makes a more congenial pet, and statistics show it also tends to live a few years longer than an unaltered one. A male neutered before maturity is far less likely to spray, wander off, or get into fights.

Although many people fear that the surgery will make their pet become fat and sluggish, this is not true. Every overfed, underexercised cat or dog is likely to put on weight, whether or not it is spayed or neutered.

*Avoid Declawing*

While there is almost no controversy about the need to alter cats, the same cannot be said of declawing. This is a subject about which many people feel strongly.

Some veterinarians do not recommend the operation except in extreme situations; others say the surgery causes only minimal pain that the cat soon forgets. The fact that veterinarians make money from this operation may color the views of a few.

Declawing is not a minor operation and can lead to serious complications. Several cat owners we interviewed who have had declawing performed say they would never have it done on another cat. The

Cats love to play with a ball of twine. Usually, this is harmless, but they *can* choke on such objects as rubber bands, pieces of ribbon, or string.

experience was traumatic for the cats both emotionally and physically.

Apart from the postoperative suffering, the operation leaves the cat almost defenseless in the outdoor world. Do not resort to declawing until all other possible damage control methods (described later) have been tried and the only alternative is having the animal put to sleep.

### Advance Precautions

Before the newcomer arrives in the house or apartment, the quarters should be looked over with an eye to hazards to be removed and precautions to be taken.
- Keep clothes washer, dryer, and dishwasher doors closed
- Electric fans should be inaccessible
- Keep stringy objects that a cat can play with and choke on—rubber bands, beads, pieces of ribbon or string—out of reach as well as small objects such as buttons that can be accidentally swallowed
- Many cat toys come with tiny bells attached; cut these off and discard them
- Cats often like to tip over wastebaskets, so try not to dispose of anything there that might be harmful, such as chicken bones or used razor blades
- Do not leave knives or other sharp instruments where a cat can land on them

In addition to these precautions, make sure all windows are screened and that the screens are secure. No unscreened window should ever be left open to a width a kitten or cat can squeeze through. Many people mistakenly believe that cats have a fine sense of balance. When they climb trees, their claws can cling to the bark, but they have no purchase on windows, balconies, and fire escapes. High-rise falls are common. They cause more cat deaths than accidents on the highways.

Few poisons are more attractive or more lethal to cats than antifreeze. They find its smell and taste irresistible. If you have an attached garage, keep your indoor cat out of it. Just a spill of antifreeze on the floor can be fatal.

Toxic materials such as household cleaners should be stored as securely as if there were a small child in the family.

Avoid or remove certain houseplants that can poison or kill a cat that nibbles on them. Not all cats go after them, but many do for lack of grass to graze on. The common philodendron is a hazard. Other poisonous plants include dieffenbachia, English ivy, caladium, oleander, and daffodils. Spider plants occasionally absorb toxic elements in the air and become poisonous to cats. In the Christmas season, it is safer to forego poinsettias, mistletoe, bittersweet, holly, and Christmas cherry.

To help keep Tabby's mind off other household plants, grow catnip. Most large mail-order seed houses sell catnip seeds, but check local store racks first. Seeds can be planted outdoors in the spring and the leaves brought in all summer for nibbling. Both catnip and oat grass grown from seeds in indoor pots provide a browsing substitute.

The reader at this point may wonder how cats manage to survive indoor life at all, considering the perils around them. First, the dangers do not compare with those outdoors. Second, most pets after outgrowing kittenhood seem to become house wise, to develop an instinct for avoiding many of the lesser dangers; however, high-rise falls and antifreeze poisoning are not among them.

### Equipment Needed

People who are looking for ways to lavish money on a cat can find deluxe models of just about everything imaginable. For example, one 1989 catalog offers a gold lamé mouse for $15, an electronic flea collar for $39, and a kitty high-rise scratch post for $95. A monogrammed cat dish for $20 costs a pittance compared with the engraved sterling silver and lead-crystal settings touted in a more posh catalog. (If you have to ask the price, you are too poor to buy them.) For the cat that has everything, the Pedigree Shop in New York offers an automatic treat dispenser your cat can operate with its paw for $65 and a larger model for $85.

We once brought home an upholstered kitty house, only to see our cat go inside once, sniff around, and never go back again. Yet whenever we set an old cardboard carton or empty paper bag on the floor, Georgie—like other cats—becomes ecstatic.

Your new companion's basic equipment needs are simple: a food dish, a water dish, a litter box, a carrier, a scratching post, a window perch, a cat harness and leash, pet nail clippers, a brush, and a few toys. A small, hand-held vacuum cleaner with a rechargeable battery is convenient for cleaning spillage around the litter box.

Whether you buy special dishes or set aside some of your own, dishes of stainless steel, ceramic, or glazed stoneware are preferable to any soft plastic such as used food containers. Over time, these can become mildly toxic, causing some cats to develop an allergy to them.

Although it is possible to improvise a litter box, it is probably not worth the bother for the few dollars saved. First, the box needs to be impervious to moisture, which makes wood unsuitable, and metal corrodes. Second, it should have a top section with a slightly overlapping inward ridge to help keep most of the scratched litter inside.

Enclosed or hooded litter boxes with an entrance hole like a small dog house may seem like a good idea to keep the litter from spilling. We originally thought so. But our cat and others we know eventually rejected it because the odor builds up inside, so we reverted to the open type. We found also that plastic liners are more trouble than they are worth, especially after the cat's claws shred them. It is a simple matter to dump used litter into a plastic trash bag—outdoors where it will not leave dust—and dispose of it.

### The Carrier: A Home Away from Home

A cat carrier will become less essential for most short rides, even trips to the veterinary clinic, after the cat has learned to walk on a leash and be at ease as an unconfined car passenger. Meanwhile, this is an essential purchase. You will need the carrier, too, for bus, cab, train, and plane travel.

More than fifteen different manufacturers and distributors make and sell models in dozens of different designs, sizes, materials, and colors. They range from inexpensive lightweight corrugated plastic containers to sturdy metal pet caddies. Other models resemble soft fabric luggage and still others, cages.

Whatever carrier is chosen, it should be large enough so a full-grown cat can stand up, turn around, and stretch out in it. It needs adequate ventilation holes. Some models have extensive screen viewing surfaces, comprising one-or-more sides. Although one might think this an attractive feature, many cats would trade the view of a strange environment for the secure feeling of being enclosed. Carriers with plastic domes are more likely to heat up from the sun, which could create a danger.

As soon as the carrier is brought home from the pet store, leave it open, place a folded towel or piece of blanket in the bottom for cushioning, and put in a toy or two. If you have some catnip, rub a little on the interior. Your cat will explore it and should become so accustomed to the carrier that it serves as a comfortable refuge away from home.

## A Scratch Post from Scratch?

When shopping for a scratching post, look for one tall enough that an adult cat can stretch full length to claw at it. Most pet store posts tend to be too small and tippy or too elaborate. By far the best post we have been able to locate is a sturdy thirty-inch-high sisal model, the Felix Catnip Tree.[12]

By examining a pet store model, you may find it possible to make your own. Carpeting stores usually have samples or remnants large enough to cover a post. Choose something tightly woven and tough. The post and base can be obtained from the lumber yard—possibly from scrap pieces. We made ours from a section of heavy-duty composition cardboard cylinder obtained free from the same carpeting store. Check the post often to make sure no nails or brads loosen and protrude, or your cat can badly injure its paws.

The best way to have a cat learn to use a scratching post instead of the upholstery is to make the post part of the kitten's play area from the first day the pet is introduced into the household.

## A Window Perch

Lying comfortably at windowsill level and looking at the outside world is more than a joy for a housebound cat; it is a virtual necessity. Making such a platform is a simple matter of nailing some soft carpeting around a ten- or twelve-by-twenty-four-inch board and fastening it atop the window ledge with L brackets. Such a ready-made perch with hardware can be bought for from $12 to $30. These usually offer the advantage of removable covers that can be laundered. If the local pet store has none, try the window platforms advertised for mail order in *Cat Fancy* magazine and other such journals.

The pet sections of many supermarkets carry pet nail clippers, litter scoopers, and, of course, an array of toys.

With your pet selected, quarters accident proofed as much as possible, and the necessary equipment stocked, you will be ready to welcome your companion and to start a new and richer life together.

Nothing seems to give an indoor cat more pleasure than to sit on a window perch and watch outdoor activities.

For young kittens, life is perpetual hide-and-seek. Enjoy. At this age, any training, except for the simplest corrections, is a waste of time.

# 3 *Keeping Kitty Healthy & Happy*

When bringing home a kitten, try to minimize the excitement and handling. It may be advisable to confine the kitten to a single room at first and until you can keep an eye on it. Kittens are geniuses at finding unanticipated trouble spots. One of these, for example, could be the toilet. Keep the seat cover down at all times because a kitten can fall in and drown. It also may chew on electrical cords.

If the youngster has just been separated from its mother, it may be unhappy for the first night or two alone and make a fuss. Give it a soft towel in a box to sleep on. Even better, wrap the towel around a warm hot-water bottle, which serves as a mother substitute.

A grown cat, when introduced to an apartment or house, must inspect every room, look under all the furniture, check under the bed, and examine any closets or cabinets left open. Once this inspection is completed, it should begin to settle down.

The litter box should be at a distance from where the cat eats, preferably in another room. Puss is by instinct fussy in that respect, refusing to feed and do its business in the same vicinity. The box should be tucked away in a place where the cat has some privacy but open access. Our box is located in a little-used closet with the door propped permanently open. Droppings are scooped out daily, and the litter is completely changed once a week. The frequency of this for other owners varies with their fastidiousness and, most important, that of their cats.

*A Time for Socializing*

Except for making simple corrections, trying to train a kitten is a waste of time. This youngster finds life a perpetual game. This is a time for socializing it, for giving it lots of attention, and for using its name as often as possible.

A young animal, after it has had a chance to become acclimated to its new environment, should be held, fondled, and talked to. Such a kitten becomes more affectionate and more interesting than one left on its own. Cats, of course, differ in personality, but frequent petting and cuddling usually soften even a naturally aloof temperament. Use patience. Never force attention or try to hold a cat when it has lost interest and prefers for the moment to go look out a window.

Most cats take about three years from birth to develop a well-defined personality if you have been talking to them and having them participate in daily life.

Play with your cat at any age. It is an opportunity to reinforce rapport. Besides, it is fun. Play is especially important to an indoor cat as a source of exercise and entertainment. After all, its opportunities to do what it does naturally—stalk outdoor prey—are denied.

Simulated hunting will be a favorite game of your pet through most of its life. Tie a knot of cloth on the end of a long cord and drag it around the room. Tabby will hide behind a chair, tail atwitch, then run out and pounce on the victim. If you, yourself, are feeling kittenish, sneak into another room, find a hiding place, make a noise, and get the cat to find you. Curiosity usually does the trick. Try rolling a small aluminum foil ball across the floor. Most cats will chase it. Some are natural retrievers and will bring it back for a rethrow. Ours is not.

Later, once your cat has learned a few tricks, these will turn into games that both of you will enjoy.

It is tempting to use a finger to play with a kitten, scratching its belly and teasing it playfully. Never cultivate or encourage this behavior because those cute kitty nips and scratches turn into dangerous punctures as the animal grows and lead to a habit that will be hard to break later.

Communication should start early. Talk to the cat. Praise it. Confide in it. Eventually you will be surprised at the key words it will pick up. Musician Carl Van Vechten's cat, Feathers, knew the meaning of *dinner* and *meat*. The words could be put into conversation in any tone of voice, and Feathers would come running to the ice chest where her meat was kept. The question "want to go for a *ride?*" brings our Georgie from anywhere in the house to the back door in anticipation.

Even when a cat does not know the words, the tone of voice soon registers. Kitty senses, for example, when you are happy with it and when you are exasperated.

By listening and watching closely, you should soon discover that the communication is not just one way. You will be able to distinguish among your cat's growing repertoire of sounds and movements and read their meaning. You will know the difference between "Please pick me up and pet me" and "Leave me alone."

On this fascinating subject of communication, a friend and neighbor, the noted naturalist Jean Craighead George, has written an excellent book—*How to Talk to Your Cat.* The cover pictures Georgie with Jean, and the text mentions some of his accomplishments.

### Watch That Waistline

Because the products of major cat food manufacturers meet or exceed established nutritional standards, there is less cause to worry about the content of most reputable brand foods than there is about the quantity dished out every day. Most adult indoor cats in the United States, like most adult American people, tend to be overweight. Obesity in cats can leave them susceptible to liver, heart, and infectious diseases as well as diabetes, joint troubles, and respiratory problems. Thin cats have fewer medical problems; they live longer and have more pep.

Kittens and growing young cats seldom put on weight, even with unlimited self-feeding of dry food. Neutered indoor animals need fewer calories because their metabolism is lower and because they get less exercise than their outdoor counterparts.

Cats like, and quickly get accustomed to, regularity. Try to set the meals out at the same time each day, and dispose of any uneaten moist food after half an hour. A kitten needs to be fed small amounts about five times a day. By the time it reaches three months, however, it should be on a three-meal-a-day schedule. Feed adults two meals—one in the morning and the other in the evening.

The activities of an individual cat may require an adjustment of the portions. As a general rule, four ounces of canned food a day is sufficient for a relatively inactive indoor adult cat; if using kibble, feed a rounded quarter cup in the morning and evening. Guidelines on the package usually suggest giving Tabby *twice* that much, but remember that for the pet food industry, fat cats make fat profits.

At about four years of age, most indoor cats put on extra weight in earnest. Once on, it is extremely hard to get off. The full-grown cat with an average-size frame should not weigh more than ten-to-twelve pounds. Such an animal at ideal weight will look skinny compared with most house pets. Check the cat's weight by getting on the scales first holding the cat and then getting on without it and subtracting the difference.

If it is overweight—and certainly with an average frame if it weighs twelve pounds or more—cut back food portions. Treats, if any, should be few and minuscule. If the animal is extremely obese, have a veterinary examination. The doctor may recommend a special low-calorie diet food.

It takes a cat a long time to lose one pound, and owners should expect the dieter to become very vocal about its new hunger pangs. One Cape Cod veterinarian who put a cat on a diet said the woman owner called him after a few days, distraught. She

Young kittens need to be fed often. Then, at three months, they should go on a three-meal-a-day schedule; at adulthood, a two-meal-a-day schedule.

said Maximilian not only pestered her most of the day but had taken to landing on her chest in the middle of the night and moaning. "Sometimes," the veterinarian said, "you have to weigh the cat's physical well-being against its owner's mental health." He suggested a compromise, a more gradual food reduction.

### Meals: Standard or Gourmet?

By and large, veterinarians say, Americans base their pet food shopping on some mistaken assumptions. These stem from the love of owners for their pets, the desire to give them nothing but the best, and the belief that the cat's tastes are like those of human beings.

Major pet food manufacturers exploit these false assumptions in their advertising to make millions of extra dollars in profits. In turn, publications that make money from the advertisements are loath to debunk them.

Even many veterinarians prefer not to risk gratuitously antagonizing cat owners who delight in pampering their pets. But if you ask your doctor to be candid, chances are that he or she will tell you the following:

1. Generally speaking, Cadillac-priced, gourmet-style cat foods are a waste of money. They provide no more usable nutrients than a lower-priced standard food of a major manufacturer. Pet ownership need not be limited to the well-to-do. Major manufacturers spend millions of dollars each year on research to develop products that meet the cat's nutritional needs. Purina, for example, which produces ten thousand tons of Cat Chow a month, has the largest cat nutritional research facility in the world.

2. Cats do not need or enjoy the variety of flavors—fish, beef, and so forth—that manufacturers tout. In addition, changing foods can do more harm than good. Stick to one standard-priced

reputable brand that says "complete and balanced" or "contains all the nutrients your cat needs for normal growth and maintenance." Commercial cat foods are already fortified with vitamins, and ordinarily, it is not necessary to supplement them with anything.

3. Some so-called nature food products may be substandard because the smaller, specialized manufacturers rarely have large research-and-development budgets for testing and quality control. As a result, some of the claims they make often cannot be scientifically substantiated.

4. People who claim their cat is a picky eater and can be fed only certain high-priced tins of food have never put their cat to a true test. When it gets hungry enough—and it may take a couple of days—a healthy cat will eat the food placed before it. It can fast for a long time with no harm done. In nature, the big cats often go days between kills. To avoid upset, though, change any diet slowly, mixing in a small amount of the new and decreasing the old gradually.

Dog food is not formulated for cats. Neither is randomly fed human food. Cats require a specific balance of carbohydrates, proteins, fats, minerals, and vitamins. They also need the special nutrient taurine, an essential amino acid.

Should you serve canned food or dry? Given its choice, a cat would probably pick the soft canned food because it tastes better, but kibble is just as nutritious. Our veterinarian recommends hard food because chewing the crunchy kibble exercises the teeth and gums and helps reduce tartar. A cat being shifted from soft food to kibble may resist the change. Just tough it out, but make the change a gradual one. If using canned food, refrigerated leftovers should be brought to room temperature before they are served. Several seconds in the microwave will do it—of course, *do not* put the tin in.

Kitten chow is specially formulated for kittens. It contains the extra protein and other nutrients needed for growth. On the other hand, labeled kitten food should not be fed to an adult because the mature cat needs a different balance of ingredients.

If you do decide to feed your cat a premium food, be aware that the nourishment is more concentrated and the food is tastier. There is often a tendency for the cat to overeat, so monitor smaller rations carefully.

An illness or geriatric condition may call for a special diet. In such a situation, follow the veterinarian's recommendations.

Always keep a bowl of clean, fresh water within easy reach. The cat may not drink much—in fact, if it suddenly starts drinking a lot, check with the veterinarian—but water is *essential* to its health. The water bowl should be cleaned daily to eliminate scum and bacteria. Use only a mild soap, scrub and rinse the dish well so there is no remainder to flavor the water.

*Health Precautions*

The majority of indoor pets that are properly looked after lead long, healthy lives. No matter how healthy the cat seems, have it immunized against infectious diseases as soon as possible. Afterward, be sure to visit the veterinarian for annual checkups, stool examinations, and booster shots for continued immunity. Regular checkups often find and clear up an incipient health problem before it gets out of hand.

Cats normally do not show signs of illness unless they are *very* sick, so it is important to be aware of the common indicators of trouble:
• Blood in the stool or urine
• Persistent diarrhea or constipation
• Refusal to eat
• Vomiting
• Excessive thirst and/or excessive urination
• Loss of weight
• Listlessness
• Sneezing, runny nose and eyes, and coughing
• Aggressiveness, constant mewing, or other unusual behavior
• Loss of balance
• Constant scratching
If one-or-more signs are observed, take your cat to the veterinarian right away for diagnosis and treatment.

Except in an emergency that requires immediate first aid, *never* try to be your own doctor. Never administer any unprescribed medicine. To do so may endanger your cat's life.

## Feline Leukemia Virus

By far the worst and most common of infectious diseases is feline leukemia virus (FeLV). This disease probably kills more cats than any other cause. As many as one in twenty of all house cats may carry this infection.

Feline leukemia virus causes many forms of cancer as well as leukemia. In addition, the virus is associated with many nonmalignant diseases such as anemia, kidney disease, and suppression of the immune system, which decreases resistance to all types of infection. The symptoms can appear at any age but are most prevalent in the very young and very old; the immune system of the young is immature, and that of the old is no longer as effective.

Cats spread feline leukemia virus from one to another through urine, saliva, and blood. It can be transmitted by mutual grooming, shared litter boxes and food bowls, and wounds from fighting. If there were no other reason to keep your pet indoors and away from exposure to other cats, the greatly increased risk of feline leukemia virus would be enough.

Symptoms differ widely because of the variable forms of feline leukemia virus. The most frequent general symptoms are lethargy, anemia, and appetite loss associated with chronic debilitation.

Several fairly accurate blood tests have been developed to detect the presence of antibodies against feline leukemia virus. A positive reaction indicates only that the cat has been exposed to the virus; a negative reaction indicates only that the cat was never exposed to the virus.

After exposure to the feline leukemia virus, one of the following occurs:
• About 40 percent overcome the infection and develop immunity
• About 30 percent become *latent carriers*—that is, do not develop the disease but can transmit it to other cats
• About 30 percent develop a *persistent infection*—any of the many forms of the disease—that is invariably fatal, usually within three years

The effectiveness of the three different vaccines that have been developed is in dispute, and each can produce undesirable side effects. In addition, no vaccine is effective if the cat has already been exposed to the virus.

As a general rule, the single strictly isolated indoor cat that tests negative has a very low exposure risk. For that reason and because of side effects, the owner may decide to chance not having it vaccinated. For some reason, multicat households have a much higher incidence of the disease. It is clear how the infection spreads from one pet to another, but how the first cat contracts it in confinement is unknown. In this situation, vaccination is more important.

The vaccination question is one the owner and the veterinarian should discuss. However, any time your cat suffers weight and appetite loss, general debilitation, repeated diarrhea and vomiting, or swollen glands in the neck or abdomen, have it tested for feline leukemia virus and follow the veterinarian's advice.

## Feline Panleukopenia

Feline panleukopenia (FPL), often called feline distemper and cat typhoid, can afflict cats of all ages, but it takes its heaviest toll of young animals. Feline panleukopenia is a highly contagious virus that can kill a cat, sometimes within a day or two of the onset of the first signs—lethargy, loss of appetite, fever, vomiting, and dehydration.

It is urgent that your cat be vaccinated against this disease and that booster shots be given annually to retain the immunity.

## Feline Infectious Peritonitis

Keeping one's cat away from others, especially strays, is the only course an owner can take to reduce the chances of a cat's contracting feline infectious peritonitis. For this disease there is, as yet, no cure, no vaccine, and not even one definitive test to diagnose it.

Although feline infectious peritonitis is often hard to identify in its early stages, researchers believe that 20 percent or more of the cats in this country may have been exposed to the virus or may even have the infection. Symptoms vary from case to case. They can include accumulation of fluids in the chest and abdomen, fever, depression, loss of appetite, weight loss, and lack of coordination.

Next to sleeping, Tabby's main hobby is cleaning up. Its tongue is perfectly designed for the job.

Contact with an infected cat is considered to be a major source of the illness. It can take many months or even a few years for a cat to incubate the virus before the disease appears. During that time, the cat can spread the virus to others, possibly through its stools, as well as physical contact.

Much has yet to be learned about this fatal disease. Meanwhile, researchers continue their quest for a reliable test and a successful vaccine.

## Lyme Disease

Lyme disease, relatively newly recognized, afflicts both people and animals, including cats. It is contracted from the bite of a pinhead-sized deer tick. At the Millwood Animal Hospital in northern Westchester County, New York, where Lyme disease is rampant, Dr. Robert A. Mavian says he has treated about 250 dogs for the malady. So far, he has found no cat that has tested positive. "Cats," he says, *"do* get the disease. There are documented cases of it. But apparently much more rarely than dogs."

At nearby Bond Animal Hospital in White Plains, Dr. Douglas G. Aspros confirms that observation. "But why cats seem less prone to the disease is unknown," he says. "They certainly get deer ticks on them. Perhaps they have a greater resistance to Lyme disease. Or perhaps they have symptoms we haven't learned to look for yet. We still have much to find out."

Cat owners should watch for the symptoms: loss of appetite, lethargy, fever, and lameness or arthritic conditions. Timely treatment can check Lyme disease in animals as in people.

"But the risk of getting it," says Dr. Aspros, "is just one more reason why cats should be kept as indoor pets."

## Cleaning and Grooming

If cleanliness is, indeed, next to godliness, the cat must be a saint. Few creatures on earth spend as much time grooming themselves. This is so true that it is safe to assume that any dirty cat is sick—physically, emotionally, or both.

Cats groom themselves incessantly not just to keep clean but also to relieve boredom. When a particularly tough decision must be made—such as whether to take another nap or to check on dinner preparations—a little washup gives a few minutes for thinking it over.

At times, the cat seems to be all rubber. It can twist itself like a pretzel into almost any position to lick itself. In the few places that cannot be reached—sides of the face, top of the head, and ears—it wets a front paw with its tongue to use as a brush.

The cat's tongue is perfectly designed for both scooping up liquids and for brushing hair. It is covered with little spiny protuberances that slant back toward the throat. The tongue contains a cleansing and deodorizing agent.

From time to time, look in your cat's ears. This pet is healthy, but black, waxy dirt can indicate ear mites and a trip to the veterinarian.

Shorthaired cats generally keep themselves clean enough so that there is no need to bathe them. This is fortunate because most cats hate the water, and the first dunking sometimes turns the mildest pussy into a spitting, snarling hellcat. Avoid giving a bath if possible.

Should some rare circumstance—such as a poisonous substance spattered on the cat's fur—make it necessary, put a rubber shower mat in the bottom of the tub so Tabby will not slip around, and run in lukewarm water to a depth of a couple inches. Put on a pair of old heavy fabric gloves and a heavy long-sleeved shirt as protection. Keeping your face out of range, gently stand the cat in the tub. With no running water and as little commotion as possible, pour a few cupfuls of water over the cat and a sprinkle of Johnson's Baby Shampoo, nothing stronger. Then, gently work up a lather, and rinse well. Be careful not to get water in the eyes or ears. Damp dry the cat's coat with a bath towel. Keep the cat in a warm place until it dries. While all of this is going on, try to soothe the ruffled feline dignity with sweet talk.

*Brush Regularly*

Regular brushing benefits the cat and is usually pleasurable as well. Branches of bushes rubbing against the cat as it walks through undergrowth perform this function in the wild.

Brushing helps remove loose hair and minimizes the amount that reaches furniture and clothes. But, more important, it lessens the accumulation of loose hair that is swallowed by the cat while self-grooming. That, in turn, results in fewer hairballs becoming lodged in the cat's digestive system. Brushing also tones the coat and skin and helps reduce dandruff.

A shorthaired cat should be brushed at least once a week, more often in the spring when the heaviest shedding takes place. For shorthaired cats, use a currycomb-type brush with plastic or rubber teeth, not wire ones. A longhaired cat needs a daily brushing as well as combing with a metal comb.

*Creepy Crawlers—Fleas, Ticks, Mites, Lice—and Worms*

**Cat fleas** are tiny black bugs that move quickly

about. Look for them around the cat's head, neck, groin, and back. They leave black specks the size of ground pepper. If you find some, put a few drops of water on the specks (placed on white surface). If the specks turn red, they are caused by fleas that have digested your cat's blood.

We have a strong prejudice against any long-term, casual use of flea collars, which contain powerful poisons. Never put one on a kitten. Never use a dog flea collar on a cat.

If used, a collar should be loose enough so that two fingers will fit underneath it. Also, it is important to check the cat's neck during the first week for irritation. Some cats are hypersensitive to the chemicals. If rawness is to occur, it will show up during the first week, and the collar should then be removed.

Accidents occasionally happen with flea collars. These can get hung up on one object or another. One night, Wendy Cubberly of Brewster, Massachusetts, rescued a stray kitten, maimed and almost starved, from beneath a dumpster behind a hotel. The kitten had worked a foreleg through a flea collar, which became embedded in her flesh. After the flea collar had been removed, the gash required fourteen stitches. Veterinary treatment of the kitten cost Wendy $100, but, she says, "Skinny was worth it."

If your cat has fleas when it arrives and you use the collar temporarily to get rid of the fleas, be sure to follow the instructions carefully and not use any other flea remedy at the same time. Then, get rid of the collar. A cat that is kept strictly indoors and walked outdoors on a lead only on pavements is not likely to pick up fleas once it is rid of any that came with it originally, but be alert for any recurrence.

Fleas spend much of their life cycle off the pet, and they lay many eggs. So, the pet owner may have to exterminate fleas in the living quarters.

**Ticks** tend to favor dogs over cats. Again, an indoor life will be a protection, but occasionally a tick is brought into the house on clothing or is picked up at the veterinary clinic. Do a tick check from time to time, especially at the height of the local tick season. If you find a tick on the cat, remove it with a straight pull with tweezers and flush it down the toilet. But if it is deeply embedded, have the veterinarian remove it to ensure that part of the tick is not left in the skin where it can cause an infection.

**Mites** of several different kinds can take up lodging on cats. The most common are ear mites, and if your cat keeps pawing at its ears, examine the insides for what will look like an accumulation of black, waxy dirt. Ear mites left untreated can eventually cause deafness, serious disability, neurological disorders, and—at the least—extreme discomfort. If your veterinarian confirms their presence, he or she can prescribe a medication that should in time clear up the problem.

Other kinds of mites cause various mange conditions. These are characterized by loss of hair in spots, inflammation, itching, and scabs. Only a veterinarian can identify the type of mite and prescribe the proper treatment.

**Lice** are much less common than fleas. These minuscule bugs are not mobile, as fleas are, but embed their mouth parts in the skin, causing itching and irritation. Persistent scratching is a common sign. Because lice multiply rapidly, the condition should not be neglected. Ask the veterinarian to recommend a safe dip or powder.

**Worms**—more correctly referred to as intestinal parasites—are common in cats and especially in kittens. A fecal check on the first and subsequent visits to the veterinarian will reveal their presence, if any, so that treatment can be prescribed. The fecal examination will identify the type of parasite because each requires a special kind of medication. Do not try to treat for worms without professional help.

*Add-a-Cat Strategy*

If you are retired and spend much of your time at home, then keeping only one cat, instead of more, has some advantages. There is a closer bonding because you are the center of your cat's attention. The food, litter, and veterinary expenses will be lower.

Because the cat is by nature solitary, the attention and stimulation it gets from human company will keep it perfectly happy. But, as pointed out

Introduce a new cat to a current resident with care. One or both animals may fluff up and hiss—or worse. Usually, with time, the hostility subsides.

earlier, if a job keeps you away for much of the day on a regular basis, consider having a second cat. Many pet owners with several cats find the interplay among them fascinating to watch. With a household of two-or-more cats, there is never a lack of entertainment.

Probably, the easiest way to assure a congenial relationship is to acquire two kittens at the outset, preferably littermates. Assuming, however, that you already have one-or-more cats and need to introduce another, how is it done? The answer is, *carefully*.

Sometimes strange cats will hit it off well right from the start. One pet owner put her new six-week-old kitten, Lucy, down on the floor. "When Lucy caught sight of Bill, who was a year old, it was like he was better than tuna fish. She adored him and followed him everywhere."

Often, however, the initial reaction between two unfamiliar cats is hostility. One or both may growl, hiss, and fluff up. After all, this could be considered a territorial invasion, not to be taken lightly by either cat but especially not by the established resident. Nevertheless, more often than not the mutual threatening turns out to be just ritual.

Do not carry either of the cats in your arms at the first encounter. This can cause added jealousy, and you may get scratched or bitten.

If a serious commotion breaks out, separate the cats, put them in different rooms with the door closed between them for a while, then open the door and let them try again.

There is no way of anticipating how long the peacemaking process will take, but the best thing to do is stay out of it. Remain just close enough to step in and prevent bloodshed. Do not give either animal special attention in front of the other, and do not get discouraged. They will soon learn, at least, to put up with each other, and chances are good they will eventually become friends.

Lovers of cats share a common bond.

# 4

# Teaching New Behavioral Patterns

Because of the almost universal belief that cats are free spirits that go their own mysterious ways, most people consider them to be difficult, if not impossible, to train. The result is that very few owners, including those who might take a dog to obedience school, would even think of trying to teach anything to their cat.

This misapprehension is unfortunate because, as a result, both owners and pets miss the fun of working together, the satisfaction of mutual accomplishment, and the unique kind of intimacy that results. Training makes your cat a better behaved companion and a happier one as well.

Both behavioral training and the teaching of tricks rely heavily on positive reinforcement. This means the rewards of praise, stroking, and treats. Keep in mind that the praise/treat principle has other uses. Nail clipping, for example, gradually becomes acceptable when followed by a tidbit. A treat even takes some, but probably not all, of the trauma out of a visit to the veterinarian.

You will need to keep a store of treats on hand. Choose something wholesome. Many commercial treats tend to be loaded with chemicals. You also want a treat that is not sloppy to handle such as chicken or turkey. We use chicken livers. To prepare, boil them, freeze the livers separated on a sheet of foil so they will not adhere to one another, and store them in a plastic container in the freezer. Every couple days, move a few into the refrigerator to thaw so there is always a fresh supply ready.

Whatever treats are used, stick to one kind. Give them in tiny bits no larger than the nail on your little finger so as not to throw off your cat's balanced diet.

*Using the Litter Box*

With a bit of luck, if a kitten joins your household, it will be at least two months old and will already have learned to use a litter box. If not, the job of getting it to do so is ordinarily an easy one because of the kitten's instinct to bury its excrement and urine.

Take the youngster to the box, often at first, just to make sure it can find the way. When you see the kitten performing properly for the first few times, "good cat!" compliments are in order.

If mistakes do occur, remember that these acts are not done out of meanness, and do not punish the kitten. The old-time so-called remedy of bringing the culprit back to the scene is cruel and ineffectual, and the emotional trauma could alienate a cat for months. If a kitten defecates where it should not, scoop up the material and put it in the litter. Take the kitten there and get its paw to cover it. Then, praise the kitten and give it a treat. Use vinegar and water for the cleanup.

On rare occasions, litter training *does* pose a problem. If a cat persistently refuses to use the box—or breaks training after using the box for some time—try to figure out a reason for this behavior. Make sure, as mentioned earlier, that the

Most healthy indoor cats take readily to the litter box, but they insist that it be kept reasonably clean.

box is not near the cat's food or its bed. Make certain the litter is being changed often enough. That is vital. Cats turn up their noses at the box if the litter is so soiled and old that it has accumulated odors.

If a cat that has been a conscientious user of the box suddenly begins urinating or defecating elsewhere around the house, it may be physically ill. Frequent urination, in particular, could signal a serious condition and calls for a prompt veterinary examination. If the cat gets a clean bill of health, then look to a psychological cause, such as stress from some unwelcome change in the environment.

If you catch the cat in the act of relieving itself elsewhere, give it a firm "no." Pick it up and place it in the litter box.

A cat that is reluctant from the start to use the litter box can be more easily induced to do so if the box has pleasant associations. Put the cat down gently in the box, scratch its paw in the litter, praise it, take it out, and give it a treat. Repeat this from time to time.

Meanwhile, keep the faith. Your cat is smart. It will eventually get the point.

Cats are creatures of habit. They are most comfortable when they have established a pattern of behavior that they follow each day. A habit, good or bad, becomes quickly ingrained.

When a cat first comes into the house, decide at once what limits you will set. For example, what surfaces will your pet be allowed on and which ones will be off limits? Some people are extremely permissive, letting their pet go anywhere and do virtually anything; others are more restrictive.

Be reasonable in your expectations, however. For example, no cat can be expected to live only on the floor, nor can it be expected to understand property rights. It may reasonably assume that an unattended chicken leg left on a plate within paw reach is literally up for grabs.

Whether your attitude is totally relaxed or, in some respects, strict, consistency is the key. It is as confusing to an animal as it is to a child to be allowed certain behavior one day and be scolded for the very same act the next.

Our own belief is that indoor cats, like children, are most secure living within a framework of reasonable discipline. Animals grow up that way. A mother cat allows her kittens only so much freedom until she intervenes to pick them up by the scruff of the neck or, if need be, administer a cuff.

Cats that have been socialized want to please their owners. They love to hear an approving voice, "What a *nice* cat! *Good* boy!" or *"Good* girl!" Compliments are even more pleasurable when accompanied by stroking and a little treat. Contrariwise, cats usually do not like to incur displeasure. A shouted *"no! . . . bad* cat!" sends them skulking off in a glum mood. Of course, given the choice between not hearing "bad cat!" and stealing a bit of meat off the kitchen counter when you are out of sight is another matter. With cats as with people, conscience has its limits.

Most cats get used to the idea that jumping onto certain surfaces— such as the kitchen range or the dinner table—is forbidden, as long as that is clearly indicated. When they try the first time, take them off with a reprimand. The "no" becomes increasingly sharp with repeat offenses. As needed, rein-

If you set consistent limits at the start, cats learn to respect bounds. If you are permissive, cats quickly understand that too.

force the scolding by tossing a magazine or some other object in the general direction to frighten the cat when it is in the midst of some criminal activity. If you go after it with your hand, the hand will become a threatening symbol. You do not want that to happen. Avoid hurting your pet, or it will become fearful and resentful. The chances for a loving rapport may be lost for good.

Remember that, to be effective, discipline must be done on the spot. If an offense is discovered after the fact, forget it. The cat will not associate a reprimand with the misdeed.

As a last resort, buy a spray type cat repellent. This could be helpful in protecting some pieces of furniture until avoidance has become a habit. While your pet is learning to stay off forbidden surfaces, it is prudent to remove breakable items and store those in safer places.

## Controlling Aggression

Even a normally affectionate cat, as though responding to some primal compulsion, may once in a while strike out at a person who is petting it or reaching toward it. When a cat is lying on its back with paws in the air, it is usually a good idea to keep your hands away from it. This is a feline's defensive posture. No matter how much your pet loves you, it may, as reflex behavior, take a swipe at your hand with its teeth or claws. Some cats never like to have their stomachs stroked.

If a cat bites—not with the gentle mouthing that is a form of kiss but a *real* bite—or if it rakes with its claws, I make an exception to the no-cuffing rule and respond instantly with a rap of the knuckles and a "bad cat!" loud enough to shake the rafters. One would probably do that instinctively anyhow, out of fury. The purpose of this is more to inflict an indignity than an actual hurt.

Our experience has been that a cat will forgive the swipe given in anger even before you have forgiven the bite. It knows that the reaction was deserved, and it will try to cozy up. But, ignore

Cats do not like closed doors—screened or otherwise.

She gives an example of how it is applied:

Two women who became housemates each brought two adult male cats with them. Each woman, of course, believed her cats were perfect. When the fur flew, it was the others' fault. They called me because the two older cats had been going at each other with such ferocity that the women had spent several hundred dollars with the vet repairing lacerations and abcesses.

They were at their wit's end. The situation had gone on for a couple months to the point where the relationship between the two friends was becoming strained.

I interviewed them. Observing the cats, I soon saw that the primary instigator was Ivy, the 10-year-old male of the woman who had moved into the house of the other woman. Ivy would stalk Jimmy and, growling and hissing, jump on him.

I discussed with the two owners the proper procedure. Whenever any one of the four cats

An open door makes a nice perch for supervising the household.

your pet for an hour or so to be sure it understands that it is in the penalty box.

If the cat, after biting or scratching, jumps away before you can react, do not chase it. You will have to settle for a scolding.

Some authorities, however, believe that even in this circumstance cuffing a cat is counterproductive. Patricia Curtis, author of *The Indoor Cat—How to Understand, Enjoy, and Care for House Cats,* writes that "the natural human reaction, when a cat bites or scratches you, is to smack it. . . . My feeling is that we should try to control the impulse; I have never yet known or even heard of a cat that was cured of any bad habit by being hit, without a concomitant bad effect on its personality."[13]

### The Isolation Treatment

Judy Newlander (an Albuquerque, New Mexico, counselor on cat behavior) has had success with a nonviolent method of punishing aggression in cats.

started any kind of aggressive behavior—just growling and hissing didn't count because that's normal—but any move toward another cat, that offender was to be isolated in the bathroom for a minimum of 30 minutes and a maximum of 45. No lights, no food, no water, no litter box, no "poor kitty," no communication whatsoever.

While I was there when Ivy jumped on Jimmy, I demonstrated the method. Without a word I picked Ivy up by the scruff of the neck, supporting the underbody, of course. By picking a cat up by the scruff, you are saying that people are dominant in this household, saying, in effect, I am the mother cat and putting you in isolation until you learn to behave.

After 30 minutes Ivy stopped yowling and screaming and scratching at the door. We let him out and ignored him. He walked up to Jimmy, turned, looked at me and stayed away. Just a couple more treatments solved the problem.

Cats hate to be isolated. They will respond better to this kind of therapy than to any sort of physical punishment.

Persistent aggression is rare in a healthy cat that has not been alienated. This kind of behavior often occurs when kittens have been brought up in the wild or subjected to stress or abuse. Recurring aggression could indicate some physical ailment. Hostility can be a symptom of fear and pain. Take your cat to the veterinarian for an examination. Meanwhile, warn visitors, particularly children, to leave it alone. Any cat bite or scratch that draws blood can result in a serious infection and may require prompt medical attention.

*Claw Damage Control*

Training a kitten or young cat to use the scratching post may eliminate all or most clawing problems. Applying a catnip spray or rubbing catnip on the post makes it more attractive.

The compulsion to claw furniture seems to be stronger in multicat homes than in single-cat households. This may be related to territorial competitiveness.

Some cat manuals suggest using squirt guns and Rube Goldberg type booby traps to discourage clawing, but a simpler deterrent may be as effective. Whenever you see your cat stretching out into a preclawing posture against the overstuffed chair, divan, or rug, shout a sharp "no, bad cat!" with a loud clap of the hands or stamp of the foot. If this fails, throw a magazine or newspaper in Tabby's direction, anything short of bodily abuse to show anger and disapproval. Then, assuming Tabby is still within reach, lift it up, take it to the scratching post, put the paws on it, and praise the cat as though it had used the post.

We know one multicat family that has gradually replaced all fabric-covered furniture with pieces that are virtually claw proof. For most of us, that extreme a solution is neither feasible nor necessary.

"Look what I found!" *Some* mischief is unavoidable.

47

Persistent aggression in an animal that has not been alienated can indicate fear and pain. The veterinarian should look for a physical ailment.

### Keep Nails Clipped

Clipping the cat's front claws regularly will not stop the scratching, but it can lessen damage to the furniture, bed quilts, clothing, and skin. Use a pet nail clipper available at pet stores and supermarkets. About once a month cut off only the needlelike tips of the nails. "Tipping" does not hurt the cat, but clipping the quick inflicts pain and causes bleeding. A light behind the nail reveals where the pale pink of vein and the quick ends. If you still have doubts about how to do this properly, ask the veterinarian to show you.

Many cats do not like to have their paws even touched, so after each clipping, give the cat a tiny treat and lots of praise. In this way, the clipping soon takes on a pleasurable association instead of being a growly ordeal.

### Teaching to Come on Call

After your cat has had time to settle in and settle down (or your kitten, if you started with one, is four or five months old), it is time to begin some basic training. Start with the simplest exercise. Each accomplishment makes the next one easier because the cat becomes more and more familiar with the following principles involved:

- You will show it what to do
- It will do what you want
- It will find compliance rewarding

Your cat will become accustomed to accepting voice and hand cues. We will suggest some, but you can make up your own as long as the voice commands are short and unambiguous and the signals are logical and clear.

Remember to keep lessons brief (just a few minutes long) but frequent (at least three times a day).

Claw damage control calls for a sharp, on-the-spot reprimand and removal to the scratching post. Nails should be clipped but avoid declawing.

Getting a cat to come when called is probably the easiest of all exercises because it takes advantage of the feline's insatiable curiosity as well as the normal desire to be near you. This assumes, of course, that you have first made friends.

The command for this should always be the same, the name of the cat and "come!" The simultaneous visual cue is a sweep of the extended right hand into the chest.

Begin with your cat several feet away but within sight, call it, and extend your hand with the treat. Puss will probably come at the first try if only to see what you are holding. If not, move closer until Puss is attracted by the morsel. Give it the treat and praise the cat at the same time. Try it again later. Use the call at meal time.

After the cat has responded correctly several times, go to another room out of the cat's sight. Call it loudly. Allow a few seconds for the message to sink in—a cat's reaction time is often slow. If your pet fails to respond, go back to the in-sight calls until that has been learned.

You will probably be surprised at how fast your cat picks up this exercise. The "Tabby, come!" should never be used to summon the cat for a scolding, to pick it up for a clinic trip, or anything else unpleasant.

At the beginning, always give a treat and praise lavishly when Tabby shows up. Eventually, give the treat intermittently but praise every time. Later, the reward may at times be something else pleasurable such as a toy, a playtime session, or a ride in the car—once the cat enjoys riding. We believe the food treat is so small that the cat welcomes it more as a token of love than as an appetite satisfier.

### Walking on a Leash

Walking a cat on a leash will add new dimensions to an indoor pet's life and new opportunities for companionship.

Leash-training equipment consists of a lightweight cat leash and a cat harness—either figure eight or H-shaped—which are stocked by most large pet stores. (A collar is not recommended because the leash then puts too much of a choking pressure on the neck.) Both types of harness come in straps of leather, vinyl, or nylon web. The web is

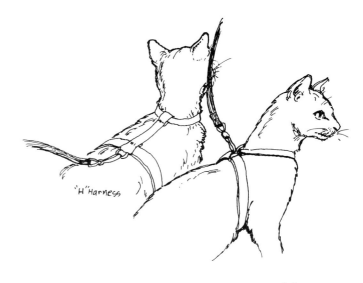

"H" Harness

Figure "8"

The author and Georgie go for a stroll. Once accustomed to it, indoor cats love this wholesome activity—note the upright, contented tail.

lightest and most comfortable. The figure eight has a continuous strap that loops around the cat's neck, crosses the shoulders, and goes about the chest, distributing the pressure equally. The H harness is formed by two separate collars, one around the neck and the other around the chest, connected by a strip over the shoulders. You need to know the cat's neck and chest measurements before shopping for a harness. If the cat is still growing, the harness can be somewhat oversized providing there is an adjustment buckle. The fit should be neither too loose nor too tight.

No cat likes a harness at first because it feels strange and confining, so the first thing to do is to adjust the harness so it does not bind. Leave the leash off for now, assuming harness and leash are not a single unit. Let the cat walk around the house with the harness on. Chances are your pet will back up, lie down, scratch at the harness, mew, and otherwise express its displeasure. Your role is to reassure the cat, pet it, and praise it. After ten-or-fifteen minutes, give Tabby a stroking and a treat, and take the harness off. Repeat this process at intervals, leaving the harness on for increasingly longer periods. Play with the cat and reassure it. It will soon learn that it has nothing to fear, and the treat will sweeten the experience.

The next step is to attach the leash to the harness and let the cat drag it around the room for a while. This process does not take long for most pets.

When the cat seems comfortable with the dragging leash, pick up the end and walk around the house with the cat, at first letting it do its own thing. Eventually, begin to guide the cat with a gentle tug one way or the other. If it will not move, walk in front and coax it along with a treat. Do not rush the training or expect too much at first. Always end each short session with praise and a reward.

You can soon start taking the cat outdoors for short walks. Here the training is easier because you are no longer working in confined spaces. It is not a good idea to walk the cat immediately outside your house or apartment if you live on the ground floor. This experience gives Kitty a strong incentive to sneak out an open front door at any opportunity. If you carry or drive your pet to an area some distance from the house before walking it, the cat does not associate the pleasure of the walk with your front yard.

At this point, teaching the cat to ride in the car should mesh well with continued leash training.

*The Making of a Happy Traveler*

People invariably say, "Oh, my cat *hates* to ride in a car!" All cats do if just plunked inside an automobile and driven off. The environment is strange, the movement is scary. If they have been in a car at all before, it has probably been only to be taken in a carrier to the veterinarian's office, hardly a happy association. Introduce a cat to car riding in stages, and it will soon enjoy this experience.

Some people believe there is more danger that an unconfined cat will be injured in the event of an accident than one enclosed in a carrier. If there is any statistical evidence of this, we have not found it.

Generations of dog owners have taken their pets for rides, apparently believing the animal's joy made whatever the risk worthwhile. The cat owner must make the same decision.

Before taking even the first step in feline passenger education, learn the two cardinal rules of safety.

1. Because a car heats up quickly from the sun—even in the winter—and because cats are easily and quickly susceptible to fatal heat strokes, *never* leave a cat alone in a parked car, even for a short time. Weather conditions can change so quickly that a car parked in the shade can suddenly be in the sun. According to the Arizona Humane Society, when the temperature is 85 degrees, a car parked in the sun reaches 102 degrees in ten minutes, even if the window is left slightly open. Just a few minutes of much less heat than that can kill your pet.

2. The other safeguard is to always make sure no car window is open more than an inch or so unless the cat is in a carrier. No matter how well-trained your cat becomes, never take it for granted that it will not jump out an open window anywhere it finds one.

The first training task is to get your cat accustomed to the inside of the car while the car is stationary so the cat feels as secure as if the automobile were another one of its rooms at home.

Cats enjoy riding if they start their experience in a parked car: first inside a carrier, then outside it.

If you have a cat carrier, put the cat inside and set the carrier on the back seat of the parked car. After a few minutes, open the carrier door so the cat can come out and explore. It may cower inside for a time, but curiosity will get the upper hand. Five-or-ten minutes later, give your pet a treat, lots of praise, and bring it back into the house.

Repeat this procedure a few more times or until your pet seems at ease in the car. While sitting in the driver's seat of the parked car, make it clear by a stern "no" and by pushing the cat away from the front floor and the dashboard that those areas are off limits. Your cat will soon get the point.

Once the cat, now wearing its harness, has become accustomed to the parked auto, it needs to get used to movement. Just move the car back and forth a few times in the driveway or once around the block. Remember to praise and treat after each ride to increase the pleasant association. Also, if the cat has a special blanket or bed, putting that on the back seat can help the passenger feel more at home.

Although it is not essential to use the car to take the cat to a walking area, the cat begins to look forward to going for a ride more quickly if that includes a stop for a stroll.

### Sampling the Great Outdoors

One of the many benefits a cat derives from being a strictly indoor pet is avoiding exposure to fleas and ticks. In view of the risk in places where ticks and fleas abound, it may be wise not to take your cat for a country outing. Instead, restrict its walking to sidewalks and asphalt surfaces. If given a choice, your cat would prefer browsing in the greenery, but exploring paved byways is still a welcome adventure away from the house.

Some people suggest attaching the cat's leash to a clothesline or some other tethering device so it can be left outdoors unattended. This entails some dangers. For example, if attacked, a cat cannot escape. There is also risk of exposure to feline leukemia or some other infection from contact with a stray cat.

For those first outdoor practice walks, select a time and place that will be relatively quiet, with few people about and little traffic. A neighborhood church parking lot on weekdays or a school ground on weekends, for example, might be possibilities. Mild to cool days are best. During extremes of weather, cats would rather stay at home.

### Walking the Straight and Narrow

It takes some time for a cat to accept the fact that you are the one who sets the direction. At first, it will want to go off on a tangent and will strain at the lead. Gently but firmly hold it in check and encourage it to walk in a straight line where you want to go. It will soon discover that the only direction it *can* go is forward with you. For this purpose, the edges of a sidewalk, often with buildings on one side and gutters on the other, form natural boundaries the cat begins to recognize.

Walking on leash requires only time and patience. Do not expect the cat to march like a dog at your heel. It will stop from time to time, sniff the air, and look around before continuing. It may even decide at some point to lie down for a few seconds. If this happens, there are two choices— either pause, yourself, for a rest or coax it along with a treat. Never try to drag it.

By the time you are driving to the walking area, the car will represent security to the cat—a home away from home. Carry the cat a distance from the car. Then, turn around, heading back toward the car. When you put your buddy down, it will walk or trot in a beeline toward its car.

Repetition, praise, and an occasional treat will do wonders. The ride and walk will shortly become treat enough. Whenever going out, say "let's go for a *ride.*" It will learn the word, and soon when you say that and stand by the door, your cat will come running.

We often have occasion to take long car trips with Georgie. When we do, we place a litter box in the back of the station wagon. Georgie shows no reluctance to use it, even while the car is in motion.

By now, you and your cat will already have set up a rapport that will further enrich your relationship and make it easy to proceed to some more basic training and, perhaps, a few tricks for fun.

After the cat's hindquarters have been gently pushed into a sitting position, reinforce the sit command with a hand signal—palm up, fingers moving from flat out to curve upward.

# 5 Tricks for Fun and Exercise

Teaching a cat tricks provides several benefits: it relieves the boredom that an indoor cat is prone to; it gives the cat exercise, enjoyment, and a sense of accomplishment; it builds a rapport between owner and cat because it involves structured repetitive teamwork. Some of the tricks to be taught are easy ones: shaking hands, rolling over, and waving bye-bye. Even these, though, require that your pet first learn to sit, lie down, and stay on command. Eventually, readers who want to do so can teach their cat more advanced tricks, such as jumping over a stick, through a hoop, or from the floor into their arms. If you follow the suggested guidelines, after just a few weeks the pleasure your cat derives from performing will be clear to see. Our Georgie can hardly wait for a chance to show off. When company is at hand, he will often without any prompting do his favorite trick, the rollover, in the center of the living room rug just for the attention and the applause it brings.

### It's Easier Than You Think

The popular misconception that cats are virtually impossible to train deters many people from even making the attempt. Yet as long as one recognizes the unique characteristics and limitations of cats, they are easy to teach.

Just as individual dogs vary in intelligence and aptitude for learning, so do cats. But the feline species as a whole has a reputation for being "quick studies." Cats not only learn by doing but also learn—to a certain extent—just by watching. Ex-periments have borne this out. For example, in one such study, researchers at the University of Nebraska placed a chunk of meat on a turntable next to a cage. The cat in the cage learned by painstaking trial and error to reach its paw out of the cage and turn the table until it brought the meat within reach. In succession, several other cats, without having watched a predecessor, figured this out in the same way. A second group of cats had been allowed to observe the maneuver from cages at a distance. They picked up the technique much more quickly than the cats that had not observed the meat retrieval process.

Most cat owners can tell stories of how smart their pet is. Georgie will run to the front door when we jingle the keys and ask him if he wants to go for a ride. This he relishes. But when he sees us pack suitcases, the cat knows we are about to take him for one of our six-hour trips. These are much too long for his taste, so he invariably hides under the bed.

Teaching a cat is similar in many ways to dog obedience training. Good trainers rely on firmness, praise, rewards, and repetition instead of harsh methods. Cats, however, are more sensitive than dogs. They are less inclined to kowtow and would, for example, fiercely resent a chain collar. One has to respect their sense of dignity and independence. Cats love praise and attention, though, and the more they get the more enthusiastic the response. It may seem anthropomorphic to claim that cats, like people, are happiest when using their talents to the utmost, but observation bears this out.

## Some Guidelines

The following are some training guidelines:
- Keep each lesson brief, just a few minutes in length—a cat has a short attention span
- Build on activities that come naturally to cats such as pawing, rolling over, and jumping
- Divide each trick into graduated steps that progress toward the goal
- Give each command in a firm but not harsh voice
- Start with the easiest tricks to accustom the cat to the methods involved in training
- End each lesson on a successful note even if necessary to, for example, nudge the cat into a rollover or lift it over a jumping barrier
- Never reprimand a mistake during a training session, saving the sharp *"bad cat"* for true misbehavior such as scratching furniture or jumping onto the dinner table
- Initially, reward each correct response, however modest, with a tiny treat as well as praise
- As a trick is mastered, give praise each time but begin to give the treat at random intervals, gradually tapering off, but *always* give a treat at the end of the training session

The hand signal for "stay!" (in either a sitting or down position) is to push the palm of the hand toward the cat's face.

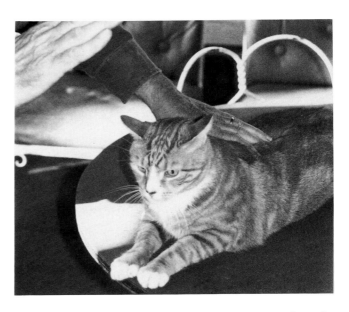

To get Tabby from a sitting to a down position, press the cat's back with your left hand. If there is resistance, gently pull the front paws out with your right. The command is "down!" with a downward motion of the right hand.

- Make sure each trick is mastered before moving on to the next

Most of the early tricks can be taught on the floor, preferably in a corner where escape is difficult, or on a table if that is more convenient.

## The Sit, Stay, and Down Commands

The commands "come," "sit," "stay," and "down" must be mastered before going on to tricks. Learning to come when called introduces the general idea of training—that is, being rewarded for giving the correct response to a human's command. However, coming at a run to get a treat is an almost instinctive reaction. A cat has greater difficulty understanding and learning the other basic commands.

To teach the cat to sit, begin by calling it, giving it strokes and praise as it stands in front of you. Say firmly in a nonthreatening voice, "Tabby, sit!" Press down on its hindquarters so the cat goes into a sitting position. Praise lavishly, just as though it had done this of its own volition, and give a treat. Do the same thing again. It may decide to flop over on its side and lie down. If so, lift the cat to its feet and try again.

Soon the cat will require less hand pressure to sit, and then suddenly it will do it on its own. When this happens, combine the vocal command with a hand signal to reinforce it. The one we use is to hold the hand out flat, parallel with the floor with palm upward, and bend the fingers up and flat again, as you would gesture someone to move forward. Give the vocal and hand signal simultaneously.

Once the cat has learned to sit, it feels its job is over and wants to get on immediately to other activities. So, soon afterwards, you must teach it to stay in that sitting position. You will not want, or need, to have your cat immobilized for any great length of time, but in order to teach it to wave bye-bye, for example, it needs to stay seated until the next command.

When the cat is in a sitting position, put your hand perpendicular to the floor and push the palm in the general direction of the cat's face. At the same time, say firmly, "Tabby, stay!" When Tabby starts to stand up or lie down, put it back in the sitting position, repeating the command "stay!" The secret of this exercise is to start with an extremely short staying time and then gradually increase it. Try to remain in a position to prevent the cat from running off while it is supposed to be staying. Indicate clearly when releasing it from the stay command by clapping your hands and saying "good boy!" or "good girl!" Pick up the cat and give it a hug and a treat.

To teach the "down" command, begin by pressing the hindquarters down to a sitting position and then gently pulling the front paws forward, saying "Tabby, down!" The instant the cat is forced into a recumbent position, give it lavish praise and a treat. Along with the vocal command, use a hand signal, which can be a strong downward movement of the forearm.

Even when the cat learns to obey this command, it seems to think about it for a few seconds before flopping down. Give the "stay" command and hand signal, and then release the pet from the down position with a handclap, pickup, praise, and a treat.

### Shake Hands

After sit, stay, and down have been mastered, shaking hands is the easiest of tricks. Give the sit and stay commands, then add "Tabby, shake hands!" or just "shake!" Extend a treat with the fingers of your left hand. When Tabby reaches its paw toward the treat, take the paw in your right hand, shake it gently, and reward it with praise and a treat. With repetition, the cat soon understands that it is the paw extension that earns the prize.

### Roll Over

Once cats learn the rollover trick, many begin to do it spontaneously as an attention getter. We combine "good boy!" with a round of applause whenever Georgie rolls over of his own accord. This has turned him into a ham, and he sometimes continues to do rollovers long after his audience has lost interest.

Put the cat in the sit position. Then, give the command "Tabby, down!" Once the cat is lying, hold the treat in your hand, just to one side of the cat's head. If the cat tries to sit up, press it down again, repeating the down command. Tabby's natural reaction will be to flop on one side and reach for the treat with a paw. As it does so, move the proffered treat very gradually in an arc over the cat's head. As it follows the hand, it will eventually roll over on its other side. For the first several times, though, it may be necessary to prod gently with your free hand. Even when the rollover is accomplished only by your push, once the cat is on its other side, instantly make a big fuss. Praise it lavishly and give it a treat. As always patience and repetition will pay off.

To teach the rollover, start by passing a hand-held tidbit from one side to the other just out of the cat's reach.

Gradually move away from the cat. Then, instead of making an arc over the cat's head, make a circular motion with your hand while saying "Tabby, roll over!" The hand signal reinforces the vocal command.

Assuming your cat has mastered all the lessons up to this point, you are now at the stage where you can combine commands. Call, "Tabby, come!" Allowing a pause for the cat to think it over, Tabby should come from anywhere in the house or apartment. When it arrives, say, "Tabby, sit!" When it sits, say, "Tabby, down!" Here a word of praise is in order but no treat because the exercise is not over. Then say, "Tabby, roll over!"

After the rollover, finish with the commands sit and stay. The cat will sit up from the down position it had assumed after the rollover. When Tabby has been sitting still for a few seconds, clap your hands to release it. Pick it up for praise, stroking, and a goodie.

Waving bye-bye is taught by having the sitting cat first reach for a hand-held treat.

*Wave Bye-Bye*

Because shaking hands is so similar to the wave bye-bye trick, which calls for lifting the paw higher and waving it, do not teach the two in succession. Separating them helps the cat understand that a different response is desired.

With about four short sessions a day, you should be able to teach your cat this charming trick in a week or two. Any cat will learn it, but some pick it up faster than others.

Give your cat the commands to sit and stay. Holding a morsel directly in front of the cat, tell it to "wave bye-bye!" If the cat tries to stand up, press it back into the sitting position. It will instinctively paw at the food. For the first few times, you may have to let the cat actually touch your hand with its paw. When it does so, tell it "good cat!" and give it the treat. Soon, hold the treat just out of reach when giving the command. When the cat waves at it and misses, *immediately* praise the animal, pick it up, pet it, and reward it. Tabby will soon understand that it is being rewarded *not* for grabbing the treat but for pawing in its direction.

The next step is to place your hand above the cat's head so that it will wave its paw in an upward direction. When Tabby will wave on command while you are several feet away, combine "wave bye-bye!" with a hand signal. Put the palm upward as you would in taking an oath and wave the fingers up and down—a familiar human good-bye gesture.

*Go to Bed and Go to Mary*

Teaching a cat to go to a specific place or person reverses the technique of teaching it to come on call. The reward is given at the destination.

Start with a destination that your pet usually enjoys. For example, Tabby may have a box or a basket with a cushion in it that is used for a bed.

Give your pet the command to come, and have it sit. No reward, just soft praise. Then say, "Tabby, go to bed!" with emphasis on the word *bed*. Point in the direction you want the cat to go. Of course, it will not have the slightest idea of what you are talking about, so lure it to the bed with a treat. Once it is there, give it praise and the chicken liver tidbit or other goodie. After doing this several times, have Tabby lie down before giving the reward.

The next step is to teach the cat to go to the bed without leading the way. When the cat is in another room and cannot see you, leave a tiny treat on the bed, and go away from it. Call the cat, get it to sit, then tell it to go to bed. If it does not go on its own, lead it over and show it the treat. Eventually, it will learn to go to bed on command from anywhere in the house. You should then begin giving your cat the reward and treat *after* it has gone to bed. Soon it will lie down automatically when it goes to bed. If you want to carry this exercise one step further, apply the stay command to get Tabby to remain there for a while, but do not push this too far. Release the cat by a handclap, picking it up, giving it a stroking, praise, and reward.

This routine can be used to teach your cat to go to any other specific place in the house.

Having your cat go to another person on command is an impressive but not difficult trick. Do not confuse the cat by trying to train it to do this with more than one person at a time.

After getting your cat to come and sit, tell it to "go to Mary!" Mary should then call "Tabby, come!" and give it a treat when it does so. Eventually, Mary will be able to omit her command; yours sends it there, but Mary should continue to give the reward.

*Jumping over a Barrier*

Jumping is such a joy to some cats that, on their own, they become impromptu acrobats. A New Jersey woman has two Siamese cats that carry this enjoyment too far. They stand on the bookcase on one side of the living room and leap clear across the room, landing on the burlap drapes on the opposite wall, where they cling. Their owner says, "We think Yin and Yang are part monkey and part flying squirrel."

All jumping lessons should be done on a carpeted floor to provide secure footing and a softer landing. The principle of teaching by easy stages is especially important here.

Start with a board at least long enough to span a doorway and eight-to-twelve inches in width. The

Jumping is a joyful, spontaneous activity for cats. Training takes advantage of their natural talent.

board should be securely propped against the door opening. Alternatively, the board can be placed across a corner of the room so that a triangular enclosure is formed, with walls on two sides; this makes it easier to keep the cat from running away.

Place the cat in a sitting position, telling it to sit and stay. Then, while saying "Tabby, jump!" tempt it with the treat to come over the barrier. At first, Tabby will almost certainly climb over the board because that is the easy and commonsense way to get over it. Praise the cat each time it does climb over, and give a treat as needed.

The lesson should be repeated several times so that the cat gets the general idea that getting over the barrier is a good thing to do. Next, make the barrier higher by nailing two boards together or using a plywood board about twenty-four inches wide so the cat is forced to jump rather than climb over it.

## Jumping over a Stick

What sensible cat would jump over a stick when it is so much easier to walk under? So, at first, hold the stick—a yardstick or a dowel or a piece from an old broom handle will do—just a few inches off the floor and parallel with it. Coax the cat to step over it with the same command as before, "Tabby, jump!" Gradually raise the stick. Tabby will try the easy route of going under instead of over several times. Each time put the cat back in a sitting position with a gentle but firm "no!" Then give the jump command again. If necessary, lower the stick a little. The cat should get the idea fairly quickly. If it does not, tack a cloth apron along the length of the stick so that it hangs down fifteen inches or so toward the floor when you are holding the stick. This cloth "board" creates an illusion of solidity. Gradually raise this. When the cat jumps over it consistently on command, remove the cloth. The height to which your cat will jump comfortably will depend on its age, agility, and enthusiasm. Do not strain its capabilities. Most young cats can make thirty inches with ease. If the jumping cat's legs keep hitting the stick, you are probably holding it too high.

To teach jumping through a hoop, begin by placing the hoop atop the board barrier so the cat cannot duck under.

## Through the Hoop

Once the cat has learned to go over the stick, teaching it to jump through a hoop is relatively simple. A hoop can be fashioned from a 64-inch length of polyethylene tubing with 5/16-inch inside

Before learning to jump over a barrier, the cat is allowed to climb over it. By degrees, the barrier is built higher.

Once the cat learns to jump through the hoop, remove the barrier, and gradually raise the hoop higher.

Going through the hoop is easy after Georgie has learned by stages to jump over a barrier on command.

The first lesson in teaching your cat to jump into your lap is to coax it from a nearby chair with a treat. Gradually widen the gap between your lap and the chair.

diameter. Insert a glue-covered 2-inch piece of dowel halfway into one end of the tubing. Then, bend the tubing into a hoop and press the other end over the other half of the glue-covered dowel.

At first the cat will balk at jumping through the hoop because the encirclement is intimidating. Start with the hoop held so the bottom is just a few inches off the floor, even if your pet has to walk through it. Then, gradually raise it. If necessary, rest the bottom of the hoop on the board barrier to block the cat from going under the hoop. Later, remove the barrier, and gradually raise the hoop.

It is, of course, important never to let the cat fall, or it will be a long time before it trusts you again.

Over the next few days, *gradually* move the two positions further apart. When reaching the point at which the cat has to jump and refuses, get closer again. One way or another, make sure the cat gets across the gap. The lesson ends, as always, with a treat and praise.

Now, it is important to make a "platform" of your hands and arms for the cat to land on. Wear a long-sleeved jacket and gloves for protection against an accidental scratch.

Stand up and get the cat to jump upward from its chair into your arms. The complication in this trick is that the cat is not landing on a solid surface and must have faith that, when it jumps, your platform will be there to land on.

As lessons progress, sit your pet on a carpeted floor directly in front of you. Stand up, bending your knees somewhat at the start, form a platform with your hands about belt level, and command "Tabby, jump!" If the cat makes a halfhearted effort and you have to reach down while it is in midair and help it up the rest of the way, just put the cat back in a sitting position and say, "Come on. You can do better than that." Give the "Tabby,

Inducing a cat to go up a stepladder is easy because it appeals to the animal's love of climbing.

### Jumping into Your Arms

Presumably, by now you will have held your cat in your arms so many times that it feels comfortable there. If not, then before you begin to work on this trick—which, by the way, never fails to impress an audience—spend some time holding the cat. Talk to it. When your pet gets fidgety, as it soon will, set it down.

Start this training by placing the cat in a sitting position on a chair or on a low stand slightly higher than the chair—the important things are good stability and traction. Move another chair close, and sit facing the cat. Using the treat as a lure, get the cat to step onto your lap with the command "jump!" At first, of course, it will be more of a clamber than a jump.

Georgie gauges the distance to the carpeted floor. For safety, it should be no more than four feet.

jump!'' command again. It will put more effort into the leap. Gradually increase the height of the platform.

### Climb and Jump

This trick builds on another activity that cats love—climbing. It employs a four-foot stepladder. We do not recommend using anything higher as we are not into derring-do and want to avoid any possibility of injury.

It might, by the way, be more difficult to *prevent* your cat from climbing the ladder than to get it to do so, but to get it to go up promptly on the command "Tabby, climb!" tempt the cat along with a treat. Then, let it see you hold the treat on top of the ladder. Tabby may make one-or-two false tries at first, getting only part of the way up, but it will quickly learn to climb to the top for the reward.

To get Tabby to jump into your arms from there, employ the same stage-by-stage process used with jumping into your arms. Be warned, though, that the cat may push off with enough force to topple the ladder, so it may be necessary for a second person to hold the ladder steady.

### Create Your Own Routines

Those who are interested in teaching their cats advanced tricks will find that cats' aptitude to learn them is enormous. For example, cats can be taught to speak, to beg, to walk on their hind legs, to walk a tight rope, to fetch and deliver items, and to do complicated routines that owners, themselves, may devise.

Readers who want to pursue the subject of training in more detail can find professional guidance in *You Can Train Your Cat* by Joe and Paul Loeb. Even more extensive information is given in *Ray Berwick's Complete Guide to Training Your Cat* by Ray Berwick and Karen Thure.

A long, graceful stretch shortens the gap and cushions the landing.

Characteristically, cats love to crawl into or lie down on anything new or different. Diva keeps Mimi Forsyth's typewriter warm.

# ⑥ Selecting Services

Of the many services available to cat owners, none is more vital than that provided by the veterinarian. When choosing a doctor for your pet, you are initiating an important long-term relationship. The great majority of veterinarians are capable, conscientious professionals who are in the practice because they love animals. Nevertheless, this field, like any other profession, has its share of practitioners who are substandard.

There are a number of ways to find a good veterinarian. One of the best is to check with neighbors or friends who have pets; another is to ask cat breeders or groomers for recommendations. If new to the area, call the local humane society or chapter of the Veterinary Medical Association, which may not want to recommend an individual but will probably suggest several names.

During the first visit to the clinic, do not hesitate to ask about the fee schedule, what facilities are available, what provision (if any) is made for off-hour emergencies, who takes calls when the doctor is away, and any other questions that come to mind.

The clinic should be immaculate. Expect to be treated courteously and your pet to be handled in a gentle, kindly way. If you are dissatisfied with a particular doctor, even though competent, he or she may not be the right person for a long-term relationship. Go elsewhere.

It is important to establish a good rapport with a veterinarian *before* your pet becomes sick or injured. This doctor will be your cat's best friend—yours too—when needed most, and you should always be able to have a full and frank exchange of information.

When moving, obtain a photocopy of the cat's clinic records for the new veterinarian.

### Cat Sitter or Boarding Kennel?

If you are going to be away from home for several days and cannot take your cat along, the best solution is to engage a house sitter— assuming you can hire a reliable person. Find someone who likes and knows cats, understands that the cat will be under stress while you are away, and anticipates that it may try to dart out a door to go looking for you.

Before your departure, the sitter should spend some time with your cat—petting it, playing with it, and talking to it. Be sure to give clear instructions so that the sitter can follow your routine of feeding and litter-box cleaning. "That's what we do," says Virginia Gordon. She and Pamela Runnell are co-owners of Critter Care, Incorporated, headquartered in Baton Rouge, Louisiana, with member businesses in several other states. They believe they have the only pet-sitting franchise operation in the United States. However, there are many professional pet sitters, particularly in urban areas. "We charge $9 a visit and stay between 30 and 45 minutes," Virginia says. "We leave a radio on for the cat if that is permissible. So the house won't be silent. We also bring in the mail, water the plants and make a security check."

If you do not have a friend who can look after Tabby and need professional help, look in the Yellow Pages under "Pet Exercising & Feeding Services" or "Pet Boarding & Feeding Services." Be sure to ask for references and check them out.

The alternative to a pet sitter is a boarding facility, called a cat kennel—not a cattery, which is a place where cats are bred and raised. Unfortunately, the great majority of kennels do not come up to standards a cat owner would hope for.

One example of a kennel highly esteemed by both patrons and veterinarians is Santa Fe Cats in Santa Fe, New Mexico. Here, the boarding facilities are an extension of the home of Sharylee Clark, who runs the enterprise. Sharylee or an assistant is on the premises day and night. Each cat is given daily attention, including brushing and grooming, and is fed its usual diet. Each of the sixteen individual kennels has its own twenty-four-inch square window with a viewing shelf beneath it. From there, cats can look out onto the hillside at birds, rabbits, and other wildlife. There are also other perches and shelves that cats can climb up to six feet in the air. A pet door provides access to individual wire-covered, concrete-floored outdoor runs, which have shelves to lie on and an overhang for protection from the weather. Each run is separated from the next by a four-inch space between the wire mesh so no cat can touch another in an adjacent run. A wire safety run extends around the perimeter of the complex so that no outside animals can have contact with the cats. This also provides added security. Should one cat somehow slip through a run doorway, it would still be confined and retrievable.

*What to Look for*

When looking for a boarding kennel, you will probably not find one with the amenities of Santa Fe Cats. The kennel industry, as a whole, lags behind cat owners in understanding what cats want and owners are willing to pay for.

There are some minimal conditions to insist on. The first is the right to visit the facility ahead of time (without your pet) and look over the premises; make sure you go inside.

- Look for cleanliness, roominess, and brightness
- Ask about cleaning techniques
- If there is carpeting, it should be of the indoor-outdoor variety that is taken up and disinfected after each tenant leaves, because permanent carpeting harbors dirt, fleas, and bacteria
- Make sure there are litter boxes and that the litter is changed daily; avoid kennels that do not use litter boxes but keep the cats on wire mesh, an inhumane practice that can cause your cat to break litter training
- Make certain fresh water is provided every day
- The cat should be fed the same brand of food it gets at home; shun a kennel that provides a standard diet for all because boarders are under enough stress without having to contend with a sudden change of food and the possibility of diarrhea
- Ask for a few references from people who have boarded cats there, and phone these people for recommendations

If unable to find a boarding kennel that you feel comfortable with, you can probably board your cat at the veterinary clinic. Here too, look over the facilities. At a clinic, cats are sometimes kept in two-foot-square cages in a dark, windowless room with barking dogs nearby, the kind of environment that can put a cat into depression.

How much should you pay for a decent boarding service? The fees vary greatly across the country, with the highest rates to be found on both the East Coast and West Coast. In the Midwest, if you are not paying from $6 to $8 a day, you are probably not getting good accommodations. Santa Fe Cats charges $12 a day, with lower weekly and monthly rates, a 50 percent discount for a second cat, and a greater discount for additional cats. In metropolitan areas, from $10 to $12 is usual, and so-called luxury kennels may charge $15 or more. One way to judge local kennel rates is to find out what veterinarians charge; if the fees of a kennel are lower, it probably offers substandard service.

*Hotels and Motels*

Once your cat is accustomed to car travel and walking on a leash, it will be able to go on long automobile trips without distress. Remember that while on the road your pet is very vulnerable to heat, much more so than a dog. (Take along a cat carrier so that, if necessary, car windows can be left open.) Also, the cat should never be let out of the car unless on a leash.

For overnight stays at hotels and motels, inquire whether your pet can be accommodated before making the reservation.[14] Many owners evade potential rejection by simply smuggling their cat into the room. In addition to the possibility of being embarrassed by discovery, there are other considerations. For example, the cleaning person can let the cat out by mistake if he or she is not alerted to its presence. The subterfuge can give cat owners a bad reputation with management, making it even harder to get motels and inns to accept pets. Before checking out, leave the quarters clean. Pet owners need all the goodwill they can get in the hostelry business.

Most cats may be a little apprehensive about the strange environment for a short time, but curiosity quickly takes over and prompts exploration of every corner, closet, cabinet, and open drawer. Before the cat is set loose in the rooms, make sure window screens are securely fastened and there are no structural openings or other places where Tabby could get into trouble.

### The RV—Rolling in Luxury

More and more Americans, particularly retirees, are roving about in RVs these days. This is the ultimate in luxury travel for cats.

Photographer Mimi Forsyth, whose four cats have seen more of the United States than have most people, describes her pets' reactions:

> They don't like the start. It takes them a full day to settle down. Once rolling, they like it. Charlie usually rides under the table (it's cool and dark there), Bear in my lap, Diva on the dashboard, Marco Polo patrolling fore and aft.

> When we stop, usually in an RV park, they're all at the windows to check on other people's activities—connecting sewer hoses, picnicking, playing badminton. They enjoy neighbors' attentions.

("Oh, look at the pretty cat!") If I stop and get out during the day, they become quite anxious. I make a point of never scolding them for anything while we are on the road. And they never make mischief either.

> When the scenery is interesting as in the forests in Idaho, they're all looking out. When it's not, as in Texas, they doze on the bed. That's how I know what's interesting and what's not.

Mimi believes that

> it's *change* that kitties don't like. Wherever they are, at home, on the road, in the hotel, they seem to have their own social patterns, who sleeps with whom, who grooms whom. I think they would prefer not being moved around, but they are very gracious about it.

### Air Travel—Baggage or Cargo?

How safe is air travel today for cats? Some airline officials and pet travel agents say there are very few problems, but others say that sending a cat by plane is worrisome.

One who describes it as "risky" is Phyllis Wright, vice president of Companion Animals for the Humane Society of United States. Since deregulation of the airlines in 1983, her office has received a much larger number of complaints about the mishandling of animals.

Rita Bott of Pinellas Park, Florida, a breeder of Maine Coon cats says, "I always worry about putting them on a plane. I've heard too many horror stories about conditions. If you have to put a cat on board, get a direct flight. And be sure to be at the airport when the plane arrives. You want to make certain the cat doesn't get left out in the sun on the airport runway."

At times, there is no alternative to air transport. There are two basic classes—air cargo and excess baggage—determined by whether or not the owner travels on the same flight.

**Air cargo** must be used if the owner is not on the same flight. The only options are a choice between regular cargo and the special expedited delivery service that many airlines have developed. All animals travel in pressurized holds with baggage and other cargo. Even if the airline does not take shipping reservations, it should have some advance notice. For example, live animals cannot be transported in the same cargo compartment with pharmaceuticals kept cold with dry ice. In general, when shipping animals by air cargo, expect the unexpected and be prepared for last-minute changes of arrangements. The following are some general guidelines that minimize complications:

• The cat must be at least two months old

• Make shipping plans as far in advance as possible

• Obtain estimated costs from every airline with flights to the destination because animal-shipping rates vary as much as 200 percent between airlines—occasionally between the rate quoted over the telephone and one demanded at the counter

• When there is a choice, choose a nonstop flight that arrives and departs during or after dark to minimize heat stress—most animals can tolerate extremes of cold far better than even moderate heat

• Ask about the airline's temperature limitations; both airlines and individual employees often differ in interpretation of federal animal-shipping regulations

• Even if the airline states that no health certificate is required, obtain one (no more than ten days before departure) just in case of a last-minute change of policy or airline; vaccination requirements vary between states

• Because animals suffer less from hunger and thirst than from the need to eliminate in closed quarters, restrict water for several hours and do not feed for six hours before departure

• Do not use a tranquilizer—its effects at a high altitude cannot be predicted.

• Have the animal at the air-cargo office at least one hour before scheduled departure time

• Call the person receiving the cat to confirm departure and provide the shipping number on the receipt—a priceless aid to identify and trace in case of errors, which are very rare on direct flights

**Excess baggage** means that the owner is on the same flight and the animal may be shipped for the same reasonable rate as other excess baggage. Most airlines permit animals to travel in the passenger section if they meet the following conditions: (a) the animal must be confined in a carrier during the flight; (b) the carrier must fit under the passenger's seat and remain there during take-off and landing. If the carrier cannot fit under the seat, the animal must travel in the pressurized hold. Inform the airline that you will be carrying an animal when making reservations—some limit the number of animals on each flight.

The Air Transport Association of America, a clearing house for all the major airlines, lists the following requirements for air-shipping kennels (carriers):

• Sturdy, properly ventilated, and large enough for the cat to stand up, turn around, and lie down

• Close securely with a mechanism that requires no special tools to operate

• Contain no more than one adult cat or two kittens younger than six months

• Display a LIVE ANIMALS label with letters at least an inch high

• Indicate the top with arrows or label THIS END UP

• Include an empty water dish accessible from outside

• Contain absorbent material (shredded newspapers will do)

• Display feeding instructions (even if they state that your pet is to receive neither food nor water)

• If any food is necessary for an especially long trip, it should be in a bag attached to the outside of the carrier

Pet stores and most airlines sell appropriate flight containers, if you do not already have a carrier that qualifies. Leave it open at home, put in a toy or two or even an occasional snack so your cat will feel comfortable in it.

If you are not traveling with your cat and need to have all the arrangements handled by professionals, there are forty-one companies located in major cities that provide this service. These firms are all members of the Independent Pet and Animal Transportation Association (IPATA).[15]

Millie Woolf, president of this group, says some of these agencies are veterinarians, groomers, or kennels, but they all will pick up, deliver, make arrangements, and provide containers. Millie's own firm, Air Animal Incorporated, in Tampa, Florida, will pick up and deliver in an air-conditioned van, provide veterinary services, and even help with boarding.

*Therapists and Counselors*

Cats are extremely sensitive to their owner's moods and to their environment, and changes can upset them. We learned this from firsthand experience when Georgie suddenly began pulling clumps of fur from his back until a four-inch strip of skin was exposed. No mites, no fleas, no physical causes were found. The condition was caused by stress occasioned by the noise and commotion created by workmen making alterations in the house. The pulling out of hair is a common feline reaction to stress.

With so many people these days turning to various kinds of therapy to solve problems, it is not surprising that cat behavioral counseling should develop into a growing profession.

Carole Wilbourne has a counseling practice on New York City's West Side. The author of several books on the subject, including *Cats on the Couch,* Carole believes she was the country's first cat therapist when she started back in the 1970s. Since then, more than ten-thousand cats have received her help. "This kind of therapy has really caught on," Carole explains. "I called myself a cat behaviorist when I began, but people thought I trained cats. What I do is deal with the animals' emotions. I try to figure out what's bothering them, what makes them happier and what makes their owners happier."

"Cats are affected by body language and the tone of one's voice," Carole continues. When she visits a cat, she records a tape of herself talking to the cat and its owner, with a background of music. "I can do this tape in such a way that when it is played back, it has a soothing effect."

Carole believes that an older person will have fewer problems if he or she acquires an adult cat rather than a kitten. If it is to be an only cat,

preferably it should not come from a home where it had become accustomed to the company of other cats.

Judy Newlander counsels cat owners in the Albuquerque, New Mexico, area. She advises them that when they notice any sudden change in the cat's behavior to first suspect a physical cause and have the pet examined by a veterinarian. "The world's best trained behaviorist cannot correct a problem that is not behavioral in its origin," she says. "For example, when an owner tells us of a cat's not using its litter box, nine times out of ten this turns out to be a cystitis situation or FUS, feline urological syndrome."

Judy, who also grooms and boards cats and has seven of her own, studied psychology in college although she majored in French. Psychology, she finds, helps her understand that some cat problems are often people problems. For example, some women say that their husbands hate their cat, so they have to get rid of it. "In this situation, it is not the cat that has the problem, it's the husband. I'd like to say 'get rid of your husband' but I can't. So sometimes you have to understand the human relationships."

Judy tells of one cat that was fed only such delicacies as caviar, lobster, and liver paté. "That cat was so spoiled it turned into a fat brat."

A common problem among companion cats of the elderly is that they are overfed. The owner sees the empty bowl, hears the cat meowing, and keeps feeding it. According to Judy, two strictly apportioned meals a day are sufficient for an adult cat. Rather than giving the cat the exercise it needs by taking it for walks on a leash along with giving it lots of love and attention, owners are substituting food, making the cat addictive. That is neurotic and it creates neurotic problems just as it can for people.

Playing with your cat at any age is important, Judy says. "Even old cats, when you dangle a piece of string with a paper tied to the end, will enjoy playing with it. They would rather have that attention than the food as a substitute."

*Cat People Pen Pals*

One of the more unusual services afforded cat

owners is the opportunity to write to one another via a pen-pal list compiled as a labor of love by Judy Hanor of Tallahassee, Florida. She, herself, enjoys writing and receiving letters and talking about cats. A few years ago, she wrote a letter published in *Cat Fancy* magazine inviting cat lovers to write to her and to give their name, address, hobbies, number of cats, and any other information. She offered to compile the replies into a Cat People Pen Pal list and send the list to all who wrote in. Judy mailed the lists out at her own expense until she finally had to ask newcomers to include return postage. The current list—she is now working on a third—includes more than seven-hundred cat-loving correspondents of all ages from all over the United States, Canada, and even a few from England.

*Befriender of Strays*

Few people return the love of cats with as full a measure of devotion and sacrifice as Judy Hanor. In effect, she runs a private permanent shelter. She owns thirty-seven cats, most of them rescued from euthanasia at the public shelter. Neutered and inoculated, they live in her one-hundred-by-seventy-foot fenced-in backyard that has a twelve-by-twelve-foot shelter. "Each time I bring in a cat," she says, "I think I just can't take any more. But I'm a softy. If I look at a stray cat or kitten, it gets adopted. I tried to find homes for them. People give you a fine story about how they love cats. Later you learn they turned them loose again."

Judy has owned cats for about twenty-five years, only a few at first. But, Tallahassee became so overrun with strays and so many cats had to be put to death at the community's shelter—hundreds each month— that five years ago Judy began taking them in. She says: "The major problem here stems from the university population. The three institutions have a combined student enrollment of about 100,000. Many of the kids adopt a kitten at the beginning of a term. They don't bother to have them neutered and when they're ready to go home, they turn them loose. Of course, these animals breed and their numbers mushroom." The city now has so many stray cats it is almost impossible to place them.

Judy gets her pets neutered and inoculated and feeds them well. She works as a secretary, and her cat food bill, alone, runs about $200 a month. "When I reach the time that I can't handle them financially or physically, I'll stop taking them in," she says. "Meanwhile, they give me a lot of pleasure. They all have their own names and personalities. When I go sit in the yard, they climb all over me for attention."

*Portraits and Poetry*

Throughout history, cats have inspired artists and poets, so it is not surprising that, for a modest fee, you can commission a portrait of Tabby in either oil or verse.

Several artists who specialize in painting cats advertise in the classified section of feline journals. One Indiana artist, for example, working from a color photograph, will do an eight-by-ten-inch oil bust for $40 or other sizes up to a sixteen-by-twenty-inch framed oil of the entire cat for $90.

Rita Bott works with the local chamber of commerce and began writing poems about people whom the chamber honored. From this, she started writing verses about her cats, which she parlayed into an unusual enterprise. People send her letters about their cats and enclose a photograph. For a small fee, Rita composes a twelve-or-sixteen-line poem about that particular cat and inscribes it in calligraphy on parchment suitable for framing.

*The Library Cat Society*

One of the most specialized cat service groups in America is the Library Cat Society. Its fifty-seven members comprise mostly librarians who have cats in their libraries as well as a few librarians who *wish* they had a cat in their library and some nonlibrarians who feel the same way. The group was founded in 1987 by Phyllis Lahti of Sauk Centre, Minnesota. She puts out a newsletter at least four times a year. One of the purposes of the organization is to encourage the establishment of a cat or cats in the library environment. It stresses the respect and need for library cats.

The group's members have some famous library cats, including Baker and Taylor of Douglas County Public Library in Minden, Nevada, who have adorned many posters and advertisements in library publications. Eastham Library on Cape Cod, Massachusetts, is the home of Melville, whose picture is on notepaper being sold in this country and in England.

At times, Phyllis says, the group seems to be facing an uphill battle because of patron criticism of having cats in libraries. Some people fear an allergic reaction to cat hairs, and others simply do not like cats. Phyllis believes it may eventually become necessary to somehow keep library cats out of the public eye.

### Cat Collectibles

There is even an organization of hobbyists who collect cat-related items—figurines, books, artwork, advertisements, calendars, postcards, paper products, stamps, needlework, jewelry, antiques, bottles, teapots, and other articles with a cat motif. Cat Collectors has more than one thousand members, most of whom live throughout the United States, but with some in Canada, England, Europe, and Australia. Headquartered in Warren, Michigan, this organization publishes a bimonthly illustrated newsletter that helps people buy, sell, and trade cat collectibles as well as obtain information about items in their personal collections.

### Help for Almost Any Problem

Cat owners sometimes face perplexing problems. As examples:

• Are you being harassed by your landlord and need to know your legal rights to keeping a pet?

• Do you need free counseling to correct your cat's misbehavior?

• Do you want to make a donation to an animal welfare group but require help in evaluating it?

Veterinarians and local humane societies are excellent starting reference resources because they are usually well informed about what is available in the area.

Throughout the United States, there are thousands of organizations, foundations, hot lines, publications, audio and videotapes, legal services, and other sources of help and information for cat owners in almost any conceivable area of concern. Many of these sources are available free or for only a nominal charge.

Each August, *Cat Fancy* magazine runs a directory of resources with addresses and phone numbers, where available.[16] The directory includes information hot lines, breed registries, colleges of veterinary medicine, and other organizations of interest to cat lovers.

"Nothing is more playful than a young cat, nor more grave than an old one." — Thomas Fuller, British author.

# 7

# Old Age & Separation

A cat that spends its entire existence outdoors has an average life span of only six years, according to Dr. Louis L. Vine, author of *The Common Sense Book of Complete Cat Care*. The cat that lives partly indoors and partly outdoors has an average life span of eight-to-ten years, but the totally indoor cat's average expectancy is fifteen years, with some reaching twenty years and more.

Scientists have learned new ways to treat the most common afflictions of geriatric cats. Good care and affection prolong an older pet's life. If your cat is overweight, you can probably add years to its life by putting it on a diet, but do not do so without instructions from a veterinarian.

The most common ailments associated with feline old age are hyperthyroidism, kidney disease, diabetes mellitus, and various forms of cancer, and it serves no purpose to describe these at length here. What is most important is to be alert to symptoms such as radical change in eating and drinking habits. Watch also for any drastic new behavioral patterns or any sudden loss of weight.

Set up a regular schedule of health checkups with the veterinarian. This is now more important than ever before. Many chronic ailments of elderly cats can be kept in check or mitigated if discovered early.

*When the Loss Occurs*

Separation and grief are a price we inevitably pay for years of loving companionship. Dr. Geis, the clinical psychologist who extolled the mental and physical health benefits of owning a cat in the first chapter, concedes, "there is a down side. I recently experienced that when my favorite cat died. It was like a stab in the heart."

In earlier days when most of this country still clung to macho frontier values, showing grief over the death of an animal was generally considered unseemly, if not ridiculous—especially so in a man. To some extent, our modern culture has changed that. Americans are now more inclined to respect the softer emotions. Meanwhile, more people than ever before have acquired pets, especially cats, as household companions. Bonds have grown closer. As a result, empathy with the grief of bereaved pet owners is far more common than it was in the past. "Yet," says Dr. Geis, "there are still people who don't like cats or dogs, who don't relate to animals at all. They can't understand the depth of our attachment."

If some friends or even relatives seem callous when you have lost a pet, try not to let their reaction add to your unhappiness. The death of a beloved cat can cause the same kind of trauma as that of a human friend. Professionals now recognize this. They know that you have to cope with this grief in the same way as any other bereavement.

Victoria Gilman, a management consultant who lives in Charlottesville, Virginia, agrees. She recently lost her seventeen-year-old cat Poco, who had been fighting a long illness that finally virtually immobilized him. "I took him to our vet of 16 years," Victoria says, "and asked him what he thought. He said, 'Well, I think if he is to have any dignity, it is time to let him go.'" She held him during the injection. "After all, I had raised him and took care of him all his life and I should be there with death. I was grateful that he could die peacefully when people so often have to go through hell." Her grief was strong and lasting. She says she was embarrassed to admit afterward that she kept wanting to hold Poco again. "But this is natural," she explains. "This has to be realized. People who say your cat was 'just an animal' don't understand that an animal gives you unconditional love. That's a rare commodity in today's world. Your pet is not going to walk out on you if you gain ten pounds or your personality changes or there's not enough money. This is a creature that just wants to stay with you for the rest of its life. It thinks you are great. And we all need as much of that as we can get."

*Coping with Grief*

Psychotherapists say that pet owners should try to accept the inevitability of an animal's death when a veterinarian has diagnosed a terminal illness and there can be no reasonable doubt about it. Avoidance of the truth or suspension of belief only makes it more difficult to come to grips with reality later.

Dr. Carole Fudin is a psychotherapist who specializes in the human-animal bond. She has a private practice in New York City and is also a psychological consultant to the counseling service of the Animal Medical Center in New York. The center provides free grief counseling. Veterinarians often refer clients having a particularly hard time facing the loss of a pet. "There is no way to avoid the pain," she says. "If you avoid it now, it can hit you further down the road. You may get socked with a double or triple loss. So I help people get that pain out."

When someone is referred to Carole before a pet's death, it is usually to help the owner cope with the euthanasia decision. "We talk about the criteria for deciding when is the right time. What is the quality of the animal's life? Is it enjoying much of what it enjoyed when it was younger and healthy? Is it eating? Is it listless? Is it in pain?"

Once you have decided in conference with your veterinarian that the merciful thing to do is to euthanize your pet, try to keep the confidence that you have done the right thing. You have given your friend a sheltered, full, and happy life. You have every reason to feel proud of your relationship and nothing to feel guilty about.

Carole Fudin says that sometimes there must be financial considerations.

> Some people love their pets so much they would eat cat food themselves before stinting on care. But you have to help these people evaluate their own needs so they don't end up in the poor house.

> One of the things we have to make people understand, too, is that their sick stomach, the lump in the throat, the inability to concentrate, the pain, are all normal reactions. Some people even have mild hallucinations. They feel their cat's tail brushing against their legs or hear it scratching. They think they're going crazy, but they're not.

*Where to Find Help*

How does one find this kind of therapeutic help? In many parts of the country, professional grief counseling is not yet available. This is a new field. Inquire of the humane society what services might be found in the area.

Lacking professional help, Carole Fudin suggests, "Try to find a sympathetic vet or vet technician, a family member or neighboring pet owner and talk about it. Talk about it a lot. If there is nobody in your immediate world you can do that with, call the Humane Society, call a cat fanciers' group, call somewhere where people are attached to their animals. What you don't want is someone who will say, 'What's the matter? It's only a cat. Just get another one.'"

Acquiring another cat immediately is not a solution some people can handle without feeling guilty. It often takes time before that decision can be made. The British Victorian novelist and poet

So beguiling is that cat that, if the need arises, an impoverished owner will usually sacrifice to care for it.

Thomas Hardy was so grief-stricken at the death of his cat that he refused to get another for many years. In the poem "Last Words to a Dumb Friend," he wrote:

Never another pet for me!
Let your place all vacant be;
Better blankness day by day
Than companion torn away.

Nevertheless, one should try to accept the fact that acquiring a second cat does not diminish the loving memory of the first. The new pet has a different personality, different characteristics. It is loved for different reasons. Far from being an act of disloyalty, adoption of another cat could be considered an appropriate tribute to the memory of the one that died.

### Honoring the Memory

One way that helps to work through the grieving process is to find a way to pay tribute to the memory of your cat. People have different ways of doing this. Some owners memorialize their pet by going through a burial ceremony, putting the cat's body in a cemetery and erecting a marker. Our opinion is that professional pet funerals can be a rip-off, but decisions of this sort are intensely personal.

Our own preference would be to honor the memory with a donation that would help relieve the suffering of other animals. Another possibility would be to work a few hours a week for a local animal welfare group—they almost always need volunteers. This would be a continuing gift in the pet's memory.

A more ambitious project would be to get together with friends and try to promote or organize a low-cost spaying/neutering clinic, assuming the community does not already have one. The proliferation of unwanted cats spreads disease and suffering at an appalling rate, so such clinics perform a vital service. The Animal Protection Institute of America supplies guidelines on how to start such a clinic.[17]

Legitimate organizations promoting animal welfare need all the financial help they can get these days, with municipal, state, and federal governments all tightening their purse strings.

But be wary. Once you subscribe to a pet or nature magazine or give to an animal welfare cause, you will find yourself on dozens of fund-appeal mailing lists addressed to animal lovers. Many of these appeals have heart-rending photos and stories designed to soften up recipients. Unfortunately, some of the organizations claiming to work for the good of animals do more to promote the good of their organizers. Be skeptical of appeals that use extremely high pressure or involve such devices as contests, prizes, and gifts. If in doubt, it is possible that either the American Society for Prevention of Cruelty to Animals (ASPCA) or the local unit of the Humane Society of the United States may be able to shed some light on the legitimacy of the appeal in question.

### Passing Your Cat Along

Occasionally, it is necessary to part with a cat for reasons beyond the owner's control. For example, we know of an instance where an elderly woman who became disabled had to go live with her daughter who was allergic to cats.

In such a painful situation, what can you do with a beloved companion? If you are extremely lucky, there may be someone in the neighborhood who would adopt the cat and allow you to visit from time to time. This arrangement might be facilitated by an offer to help with the costs of keeping the cat. In canvassing friends and relatives, try to find people who, you are confident, will give your pet affection and a good home. Get an assurance from them that if for any reason they later find they cannot keep the cat they will let you know and *you* will take the responsibility of placing it elsewhere. Otherwise, you may never know where your friend winds up.

One thing to be careful about is advertising in the local paper that your cat is available "free to a good home." There are people who acquire animals under false pretenses this way and sell them to experimental laboratories. Either know or check carefully who Tabby's new owners will be.

Failing any other safe solution, you might try to place your cat in a "no kill" shelter. Ask your veterinarian or the humane society to help you locate one. These shelters keep animals until a home can be found for them. They also tend to fill up fast and have waiting lists, so the process could take some time.

*Providing for Tabby*

Many older people worry—and often with good reason—about what will happen when they are no longer around to look after their pets. Who will care for them? Will they be properly fed, housed, and loved?

Lawrence Goodman, an attorney in Pleasantville, New York, and an ardent animal lover, says, "A cat, even though it is a loved one, is considered chattel—personal property—in the eyes of law. You will want to find a close friend whom you can trust. You should specify in your will that you are leaving the cat to Mary Smith along with a specified sum of money for the cat's care. This is called a 'precatory bequest.' It means, in effect, 'please take care of' but it is not legally binding. You can only hope that Mary Smith will not dispose of the cat and make off with the money. If she is a true friend, of course, she won't." Goodman says there is a history of large sums of money being left in trust for animals. "But, in practical terms, no one is going to know how the animal lives or dies. No one will audit the account and see that it's carried out. Ultimately the commonsense thing is to leave the cat and some money in the hands of a friend."

There are many precedents for bequests to cats. The famed letter writer Lord Chesterfield left an annuity for his cat. In 1702 when Frances Teresa Stewart, Duchess of Richmond and Lennox, was buried in Westminster Abbey, it was learned she bequeathed sums to women friends to care for her cats. This inspired Alexander Pope to write the famous line, "Die, and endow a college or a cat."

Even in the most domesticated pussycat, an element of the tiger remains.

**SADIE**

Reprinted with special permission from *Cat Fancy* Magazine, January, 1987. Copyright by David Enders Tripp.

# 8 How to Train Your Person

## An Afterword to Cats by Georgie

*Editor's note. Our own companion, Georgie, as usual has the last word. He gives your pet some candid cat-to-cat advice. This is material you may prefer not to have your cat get its paws on.*

Training a person is much easier than you would think. Even though a human being is not as smart as a cat, it is not as dumb as most dogs. People *can* learn.

You will need patience, of course, especially at the beginning. As a general rule, remember that human beings usually respond to a show of affection, like a head nuzzle, a rub against their legs or a lap cuddle. Save the nip or the scratch for punishment of bad behavior. Bad behavior is when a person does something to you that you do not want, like picking you up when you would rather be down or putting you down when you want to stay up.

Gentle people are easier to train than grouches. If you are a stray looking for a good home, keep that in mind. Also, adopt people who can afford to give you two squares a day and keep you in comfort. You certainly do not want to have to go hunt for a living. I've been out there. And I can tell you it's a jungle.

Once you are in the house or apartment, study your human being closely. No two of them are alike.

There are some basic things you will want to teach your person.

• Your meals are *most* important and must always be served on time if not earlier
• Your litter box must be kept clean
• You must get your regular sixteen hours of nap time a day, but when you are awake, you expect to be the center of attention

### Sing the Starvation Blues

There is only one way to make sure you get fed at mealtime—or sooner, if possible. That is to start making a fuss way in advance. How much ahead of time depends on your stamina. I usually start about 3:30 in the afternoon for my 5:00 feeding. I begin by scratching the door of the cabinet where the food is kept and giving a few sad meows. That never does any good, but it sets the stage, so to speak, for some real caterwauling.

You can snake in and out of the legs of your person. Make hungry cries while you do this. Otherwise, the person might trip and come crashing down on you. Always remember that people have only two feet. They are not as nimble as we are.

There are many ways to get your sleeper up for breakfast as early as possible. Try sitting on the bed next to the person's head and staring into the closed eyes. If that does not work, walking up and down them on the bed usually gets a reaction. Sometimes a violent one.

Whenever you hear the refrigerator door being opened, if you run into the kitchen and stand in front of the "fridge" and you look pathetic, you just may be able to teach the person to give you a treat. I have never been that lucky. They are tough in this house. But if you live with a nicer person, that might work.

Being placed on a diet, I found, is the most terrible experience you can have. You will be sure you are starving to death, and you probably are. I have a friend Jeremy, in California, who had the answer to that. He put on so much weight so fast—he's now a twenty-five pounder—that, he says, his people are too afraid of him to put him on a diet.

## Enforce Discipline

Teaching your person to keep your litter box clean is simple. The first time the box gets disgusting leave a deposit just outside it as a reminder. It this happens again, put the notice on the living room rug. That is usually enough to make the point.

Most people will not bother you while you are sleeping. But to be sure of this, give your friend lots of attention and quality time between your naps. For example, if work at the desk is going on, leap up and lie on the papers. Jump into the lap when the person is reading. If he or she is on the telephone, paw at a leg for attention. If nothing else seems to work, knock over a wastebasket. That makes a nice loud clatter.

If people annoy you—if little persons, for example, chase you around the house—a loud hiss will usually scare them off. Otherwise, you will have to go under the bed.

## Games People Can Play

People lead dull lives. They are always doing boring things that they call "work." So teaching your person to play is important. Teach the simple games first.

**Surprise!** That's the easiest because you do all the work. Just hide on a mantel or behind a bookcase and suddenly jump out in front of the person. If you yowl at the same time, that makes it even better.

**Find the pussycat.** This is fun because you can combine it with a nap. Make it easy at the start. Find a spot way in the back of an upstairs closet and curl up and go to sleep. When you hear a voice calling your name, don't come out. Pretty soon people will get all excited and run around the house trying to find you. This will give them exercise. When they do find you, they will be so happy they will pick you up and maybe even give you a treat.

Next time hide in a harder place. If you can get into the attic and crawl down between the partitions, people will go crazy looking for you. Then you can howl and pretend you can't get out. That is even more fun.

**Advanced training.** You can train your person to give you special treats by doing a few simple-minded tricks like rolling over, waving bye-bye, and sitting up. Jumping over a stick or through a hoop really impresses people.

But watch out. Persons are sneaky. Soon when you do your trick, they don't make good with the treat. They think you will be satisfied with a "nice cat" or some other cheap compliment. Don't let them get away with that. Make it a rule: no treat, no trick.

## One Last Word

Above all, fellow pussycats, you have to be firm with persons. Frown at them now and then. Otherwise, they may get the idea that *they* are running the house.

That's all for now. Happy naps and washups.

# End Notes

1. Dorothy Canfield Fisher, "Why I Like Cats Better Than Dogs," in *Cats and Cats: Great Cat Stories of Our Day*, ed. Francis E. Clarke (New York: Macmillan, 1937), 59.

2. William Lyon Phelps, "Essay," in *Cats and Cats: Great Cat Stories of Our Day*, ed. Francis E. Clarke (New York: Macmillan, 1937), 147.

3. "Topics—Cats," *The New York Times*, January 16, 1986, editorial page.

4. James Boswell, *Boswell's Life of Johnson*, London: Oxford University Press, 1924, 2: 478.

5. Theophile Gautier, *La Menagerie Intime*, quoted in Christabel Aberconway, *A Dictionary of Cat Lovers* (London: Michael Joseph, 1949), 152.

6. Boswell, *Johnson*, 2: 478.

7. Mark Patinkin, "Whose Best Friend Can These Cats Claim to Be?" *Providence Journal*, July 28, 1988.

8. Further information about the program may be obtained from a participating humane society or by writing to Purina Pets for People Program, Checkerboard Square, St. Louis, Missouri 63164.

9. Write to Cat Fanciers' Association, Inc., 1309 Allaire Avenue, Ocean, New Jersey 07712. For information about other registered breeds (many also registered by the CFA), write to International Cat Association, Inc., P. O. Box 2684, Harlingen, Texas 78551.

10. Mark Twain, "Letter to *St. Nicholas Magazine*, quoted in Christabel Aberconway, *A Dictionary of Cat Lovers* (London: Michael Joseph, 1949), 397.

11. Send a stamped, return envelope to Animal Protection Institute of America, P. O. Box 22505, Sacramento, California 95822.

12. Made by Felix, 3623 Fremont Avenue N., Seattle, Washington 98103.

13. Patricia Curtis, *The Indoor Cat—How to Understand, Enjoy, and Care for House Cats* (New York: Doubleday, 1981), 124.

14. Gaines, the pet food manufa urer, publishes a directory of more than seven-thousand hotels and motels that welcome pets. You can get a copy of *Touring with Towser* (mention the title) by sending a check or money order for $1.50 to Pet Care Booklets, Gaines Professional Services, Department CF, P. O. Box 877, Young America, Minnesota 55399.

15. You can locate the nearest service by looking in the Yellow Pages under Pet Transportation or Kennels or by writing to IPATA, P. O. Box 129, Arvada, Colorado 80001.

16. Nonsubscribers can access this directory through a back issue (check the library) or by writing to Fancy Publications, CF Back Issues, P. O. Box 6050, Mission Viejo, California 92690.

17. Animal Protection Institute of America, P. O. Box 22505, Sacramento, California, 95822.

# Selected Bibliography

Aberconway, Christabel. *A Dictionary of Cat Lovers*. London: Michael Joseph, 1949.

Allaby, Michael. *Your Cat's First Year*. New York: Simon and Schuster, 1985.

Beadle, Muriel. *The Cat*. New York: Simon and Schuster, 1977.

Berwick, Ray, and Thure, Karen. *Ray Berwick's Complete Guide to Training Your Cat*. Tucson, Arizona: HP Books, 1986.

Boswell, James. *Boswell's Life of Johnson*. Lon don: Oxford University Press, 1924.

Clarke, Frances E., ed. *Cats and Cats: Great Cat Stories of Our Day*. New York: Macmillan, 1937.

Curtis, Patricia. *The Indoor Cat—How to Understand, Enjoy, and Care for House Cats*. New York: Doubleday, 1981.

Dale-Green, Patricia. *Cult of the Cat*. Boston: Houghton Mifflin, 1963.

Fisher, Dorothy Canfield. "Why I Like Cats Better Than Dogs." In *Cats and Cats: Great Cat Stories of Our Day*, edited by Francis E. Clarke. New York: Macmillan, 1937.

Fogarty, Marna Sharon. *The Cat Yellow Pages*. New York: Charles Scribner's Sons, 1984.

Fox, Michael W. *Understanding Your Cat*. New York: Coward, McCann and Geoghegan, 1974.

George, Jean Craighead. *How to Talk to Your Cat*. New York: Warner, 1986.

Joseph, Michael. *Cat's Company*. New York: Dodd Mead and Company, 1931.

Loeb, Joe, and Loeb, Paul. *You Can Train Your Cat*. New York: Simon and Schuster, 1977.

Patinkin, Mark. "Whose Best Friend Can These Cats Claim to Be?" *Providence Journal*, July 28, 1988.

Phelps, William Lyon. "Essay." In *Cats and Cats: Great Cat Stories of Our Day*, edited by Francis E. Clarke. New York: Macmillan, 1937.

Pond, Grace. *The Cat—The Breeds, the Care and the Training*. New York: Exeter Books, 1984.

Sillar, F. C., and Meyler, Ruth M. *Cats Ancient and Modern*. New York: Viking Press, 1966.

Stuart, Dorothy Margaret. *A Book of Cats, Literary, Legendary, and Historical*. London: Methuen, 1959.

"Topics—Cats." *The New York Times*, January 16, 1986, editorial page.

Vine, Louis L. *The Common Sense Book of Complete Cat Care*. New York: William Morrow and Company, 1978.

Wilbourne, Carole. *Cats on the Couch: The Complete Guide for Loving and Caring for Your Cat*. New York: Humane Society, 1988.

# Index